Apress Pocket Guides

Apress Pocket Guides present concise summaries of cutting-edge developments and working practices throughout the tech industry. Shorter in length, books in this series aims to deliver quick-to-read guides that are easy to absorb, perfect for the time-poor professional.

This series covers the full spectrum of topics relevant to the modern industry, from security, AI, machine learning, cloud computing, web development, product design, to programming techniques and business topics too.

Typical topics might include:

- A concise guide to a particular topic, method, function or framework

- Professional best practices and industry trends

- A snapshot of a hot or emerging topic

- Industry case studies

- Concise presentations of core concepts suited for students and those interested in entering the tech industry

- Short reference guides outlining 'need-to-know' concepts and practices.

More information about this series at https://link.springer.com/bookseries/17385.

Cybersecurity Threats and Attacks in the Gaming Industry

Secure Game Players' and Developers' Data and Systems

Massimo Nardone

Apress®

Cybersecurity Threats and Attacks in the Gaming Industry: Secure Game Players' and Developers' Data and Systems

Massimo Nardone
Helsinki, Finland

ISBN-13 (pbk): 979-8-8688-1491-4   ISBN-13 (electronic): 979-8-8688-1492-1
https://doi.org/10.1007/979-8-8688-1492-1

Managing Director, Apress Media LLC: Welmoed Spahr
Acquisitions Editor: Spandana Chatterjee
Editorial Assistant: Gryffin winkler

Cover designed by eStudioCalamar

Distributed to the book trade worldwide by Springer Science+Business Media New York, 1 New York Plaza, New York, NY 10004. Phone 1-800-SPRINGER, fax (201) 348-4505, e-mail orders-ny@springer-sbm.com, or visit www.springeronline.com. Apress Media, LLC is a Delaware LLC and the sole member (owner) is Springer Science + Business Media Finance Inc (SSBM Finance Inc). SSBM Finance Inc is a **Delaware** corporation.

For information on translations, please e-mail booktranslations@springernature.com; for reprint, paperback, or audio rights, please e-mail bookpermissions@springernature.com.

Apress titles may be purchased in bulk for academic, corporate, or promotional use. eBook versions and licenses are also available for most titles. For more information, reference our Print and eBook Bulk Sales web page at http://www.apress.com/bulk-sales.

If disposing of this product, please recycle the paper

This book is dedicated to the memory of my loving late father Giuseppe. Your support, your education, your values made me the man I am now. You will be loved and missed forever.

I also would like to dedicate this book to my children Luna, Leo, and Neve. Your love and support mean everything to me.

—Massimo

Table of Contents

About the Author

Massimo Nardone has more than 29 years of experience in information and cybersecurity for IT/OT/IoT/IIoT, web/mobile development, cloud, and IT architecture. His true IT passions are security and Android. He holds an MSc in Computing Science from the University of Salerno, Italy. Throughout his working career, he has held various positions, starting as a programming developer, and then security teacher, PCI QSA, auditor, assessor, lead IT/OT/SCADA/cloud architect, CISO, BISO, executive, program director, OT/IoT/IIoT security competence leader, VP OT security, etc. In his last working engagement, he worked as a seasoned cyber and information security executive, CISO and OT, IoT and IIoT security competence leader helping many clients to develop and implement cyber, information, OT, and IoT security activities. He is currently working as Vice President of OT Security for SSH Communications Security. He is author of the following Apress books Cybersecurity Threats & Attacks in the Gaming Industry, Spring Security 6 Recipes, Secure RESTful APIs as well as co-author of numerous Apress books, including *Pro Spring Security, Pro JPA 2 in Java EE 8*, and *Pro Android Games*, and has reviewed more than 80 titles.

About the Technical Reviewer

Anna Rosa Lappalainen is a Finnish entrepreneur and technology executive with a career in gaming and tech startups. She is the Co-founder and Chief Operating Officer of Return Entertainment, a Helsinki-based company building a cloud-native gaming platform and games for mainstream TV audiences.

With a career spanning over two decades, Lappalainen has held pivotal roles in various organizations. She co-founded Vizor.io, a WebVR content creation platform, where she served as COO. Her professional journey also includes positions such as Senior Project Manager at Valve, Product Manager at Properazzi, and Project Manager at Splice music, where she helped create and build innovative and groundbreaking games, technologies, and services.

Academically, Lappalainen holds a master's degree in Cultura Històrica, Comunicació i Noves Professions from the Universitat de Barcelona and an MSc in International Economics, French language, and Econometrics from Aalto University.

Beyond her professional endeavors, she is recognized for her multilingual abilities, speaking nine languages, and her active participation in the Finnish startup community.

For more insights into her work and perspectives, Lappalainen has been featured in interviews and podcasts discussing startups, networking, and the evolving landscape of technology and gaming.

Acknowledgments

Many thanks go to my wonderful children Luna, Leo, and Neve for your continuous support. You are and will be always the most beautiful reason of my life.

I want to thank my beloved late father Giuseppe and my mother Maria, who always supported me and loved me so much. I will love and miss both of you forever.

Thanks also to my beloved brothers, Roberto and Mario, for your endless love and for being the best brothers in the world and to Brunaldo and Kaisa for bringing joy and happiness to Luna and Leo.

Thanks a lot to Spandana Chatterjee for giving me the opportunity to work as writer on this book, to Krishnan Sathyamurthy for doing such a great job during the editorial process and supporting me all the time, and of course to Anna Rosa Lappalainen, the technical reviewer of this book, for helping me to make a better book.

Introduction

Cybersecurity is a critical concern in the gaming industry due to the significant financial investments, personal data, and intellectual property at stake. Game developers, publishers, and players all have a vested interest in maintaining a secure gaming environment.

This book is about cybersecurity in the gaming industry, which is essential to protect player data, maintain a secure gaming environment, and safeguard intellectual property.

The book will consider both players and game developers and how and why they need to remain vigilant, educate themselves about potential threats, and employ best practices to ensure a safe and enjoyable gaming experience.

We will start by introducing cybersecurity in the gaming industry, and then, we will concentrate on data privacy and protection of game user data, showing why securing data is essential, but not only, in the gaming industry.

You will learn about cybersecurity, the most common and known threats and attacks in the gaming industry, why attacks in the gaming industry are executed, and the reasons behind that.

The book will then explain the key IT architecture elements of cybersecurity in the gaming industry. As an advanced game developer, you would want to know the IT architecture elements to be considered when designing games.

Of course, there are also important security standards, frameworks, and regulations in the gaming industry which are needed to be also well understood.

This book will provide a lot of game examples and use cases about different game types like mobile games, TV games, web games, etc.

At the end of this book, you will learn how to secure the game environments and its best practices.

CHAPTER 1

Introduction to Cybersecurity in the Gaming Industry

Cybersecurity is a critical concern in the gaming industry due to the significant financial investments, personal data, and intellectual property at stake. Game developers, publishers, and players all have a vested interest in maintaining a secure gaming environment.

Cybersecurity in the gaming industry is essential to protect player data, maintain a secure gaming environment, and safeguard intellectual property. Both players and game developers need to remain vigilant, educate themselves about potential threats, and employ best practices to ensure a safe and enjoyable gaming experience.

This pocketbook will explain the critical role of cybersecurity in the gaming industry, the unique challenges it faces, and the strategies employed to mitigate risks.

© Massimo Nardone 2025
M. Nardone, *Cybersecurity Threats and Attacks in the Gaming Industry*, Apress Pocket Guides, https://doi.org/10.1007/979-8-8688-1492-1_1

Why Cybersecurity Matters in the Gaming Industry?

Cybersecurity in gaming is essential for maintaining trust among players, protecting investments, and ensuring a safe and enjoyable gaming environment.

Listed here are the major reasons why cybersecurity matters in the gaming industry:

- **Massive User Base:**
  Online gaming platforms host millions of players globally, collecting vast amounts of personal information, including names, email addresses, and payment details. These data sets are prime targets for cybercriminals.

- **High Revenue Potential:**
  With the rise of microtransactions, subscription services, and esports, the gaming industry generates billions of dollars annually. This financial aspect makes it a tempting target for attackers seeking to exploit vulnerabilities for monetary gain.

- **Complex Ecosystem:**
  Gaming involves diverse stakeholders, including developers, publishers, platforms, and players. Each layer of this ecosystem introduces potential vulnerabilities, from server-side exploits to client-side hacks.

- **Reputation and Trust:**
  For gaming companies, maintaining a secure environment is crucial for user trust. A single data breach or hacking incident can damage a company's reputation and lead to player attrition.

Let's introduce now the different categories of games in order to understand better the cybersecurity risks involved.

Categories of Games and the Risks Involved

Different types of games categorized by the platforms or methods used to play them present distinct features, experiences, and cybersecurity challenges.

We must understand the different categories of games helping in tailoring cybersecurity measures to each platform's unique vulnerabilities and user base.

Typically, the categories of the type of games are divided as follows:

- **Console games**

- **Browser games**

- **PC games**

- **Downloaded games**

- **Mobile games**

Let's explore them!

Console Games

Console games are video games designed specifically to be played on gaming consoles dedicated hardware systems built for gaming. These consoles connect to a display (such as a TV or monitor) and often come with proprietary controllers for gameplay. Console games are one of the most popular forms of gaming, offering high-quality graphics, immersive experiences, and access to exclusive titles.

Console gaming remains a dominant force in the industry, offering a unique blend of accessibility, exclusive content, and cutting-edge technology.

The most common dedicated gaming console platforms are PlayStation, Xbox, and Nintendo Switch.

The most important features of console game are as follows:

1. **Dedicated Gaming Hardware**

   - Consoles are purpose-built for gaming, providing optimized performance for their supported games. Examples of popular consoles include

     - **PlayStation** (Sony)

     - **Xbox** (Microsoft)

     - **Nintendo Switch** (Nintendo)

   - Each console has unique hardware and controller designs.

2. **High-Quality Graphics and Performance**

   - Modern consoles support advanced graphical capabilities, including 4K resolution, ray tracing, and HDR.

   - Games are developed to run efficiently on specific console hardware, ensuring stable performance.

3. **Exclusive Titles**

   - Console manufacturers often secure exclusive games (e.g., *The Legend of Zelda* for Nintendo, *God of War* for PlayStation) to attract players to their platforms.

4. **Physical and Digital Distribution**

   - Console games are available in two formats:

     - **Physical Discs**: Purchased from retailers.

- **Digital Downloads**: Acquired from online storefronts like PlayStation Store, Xbox Marketplace, or Nintendo eShop.

5. **Online Connectivity**

    - Most consoles provide online services for multiplayer gaming, digital storefronts, and cloud saves. Examples include

        - PlayStation Network (PSN)

        - Xbox Live

        - Nintendo Switch Online

    - Some services require subscriptions for online play and additional perks.

6. **Plug-and-Play Experience**

    - Consoles offer a straightforward setup: plug them into a TV or monitor, insert a game or download one, and start playing.

    - They do not require the extensive customization or system requirements that PC gaming often entails.

Popular Console Game Genres in 2024 include (source Statista)

- **Action games**

- **Adventure games**

- **Role-playing games (RPGs)**

- **Battle royale games**

- **Simulation games**

- **Puzzle and brain games**

These genres not only provide entertainment but also reflect the evolving preferences of gamers, showcasing the industry's ability to innovate and adapt to new trends.

Based to Newzoo source, in 2024, the console gaming market saw several standout titles achieving remarkable sales and popularity across different regions:

1. **Fortnite: The King Still Reigns**

2. **Minecraft: Block by Block, Still on Top**

3. **Call of Duty: Warzone. The Fast and Furious of FPS**

4. **League of Legends: Old but Gold**

5. **Valorant: Where Superpowers Meet Sharpshooters**

6. **Genshin Impact**

7. **Roblox**

8. **Apex Legends**

Cybersecurity Concerns in Console Games

While console ecosystems are relatively secure compared to open systems like PCs, they still face cybersecurity risks which involve in general:

- Hacking of user accounts tied to online subscriptions or marketplaces

- Unauthorized modifications to firmware or software

- Phishing attempts targeting players in multiplayer environments

More specifically, console game cybersecurity risks include

- **Account Theft:** Players' accounts often store payment details and purchased games, making them targets for hackers.

- **Phishing Scams:** Fake messages or websites mimicking official services can trick users into sharing credentials.

- **Firmware Exploits:** Unauthorized modifications to console firmware can allow piracy but also make the system vulnerable to malware.

- **DDoS Attacks:** Online services and game servers can be disrupted, preventing players from accessing multiplayer features.

- **In-Game Scams and Fraud:** Multiplayer and in-game economies are susceptible to scams and fraud.

Browser Games

Browser games are video games that can be played directly within a web browser without the need for downloading or installing additional software. These games leverage web technologies like **HTML5**, **WebGL**, **JavaScript**, or older technologies like **Flash** (now deprecated) to deliver interactive experiences. They are accessible on various devices, including PCs, tablets, and smartphones, making them highly convenient for casual and quick gaming sessions.

Browser games are played directly in web browsers (e.g., Chrome, Firefox) using technologies like HTML5, WebGL, and JavaScript.

General features of browser games include the following:

- No downloads required; accessible instantly through URLs

- Often lightweight, with simpler graphics and mechanics compared to console or PC games

- Includes casual games, social games, and some multiplayer options

The most important features of browser games are

1. **No Installation Required**

    - Players can start playing instantly by navigating to a URL, without the need to download or install anything.

2. **Cross-platform Accessibility**

    - Since they run in browsers, these games are often platform-agnostic, working on Windows, macOS, Linux, or mobile operating systems like Android and iOS.

3. **Wide Variety of Genres**

    - Browser games cover genres like puzzles, strategy, RPGs, simulation, multiplayer online games (MMOs), and more.

4. **Casual and Lightweight**

    - Many browser games are designed to be quick and easy to play, often requiring minimal time commitment.

5. **Free-to-Play Model**

- Most browser games are free, with revenue generated through ads, in-game purchases, or subscriptions for premium content.

6. **Multiplayer Options**

- Some browser games, like *Agar.io* or *Slither.io*, offer real-time multiplayer experiences, allowing players to compete or collaborate with others online.

Based on Newzoo source, in 2024, browser games continued to captivate a broad audience, with several genres standing out in popularity including

- **Battle royale games**

- **Role-playing games (RPGs)**

- **Puzzle and brain games**

The top three browser games played in 2024 were (source Newzoo)

1. Hamster Kombat: `https://hamsterkombatgame.io/`

2. GeoGuessr: `https://www.geoguessr.com/`

3. Infinite Craft: `https://infinite-craft.com/`

Cybersecurity Concerns in Browser Games

Browser games, while convenient and accessible, come with specific cybersecurity risks due to their reliance on web technologies and minimal installation barriers.

Cybersecurity risks generally include

- Risk of malicious advertisements or pop-ups

- Phishing sites mimicking popular games

- Exploitation of browser vulnerabilities

- Data collection and tracking by unverified sites

More specifically, browser game cybersecurity risks, which can compromise player data, devices, and even broader systems, include

- **Malware and Malicious Code:** Some browser games, especially from unverified sources, may contain malicious code.

- **Phishing Attacks:** Players may be targeted through in-game messages, fake login pages, or pop-ups.

- **Unsecured Data Transmission:** Browser games without HTTPS or secure protocols may transmit user data in plaintext.

- **Insecure Ads and Pop-Ups:** Many browser games are ad-supported, and these ads may contain malicious code.

- **Exploitation of Browser Vulnerabilities:** Outdated or insecure browsers may have vulnerabilities that attackers exploit through browser games.

- **Data Privacy Issues:** Many browser games collect player data for advertising or analytics.

- **DDoS Attacks:** Browser game servers, especially multiplayer ones, are prone to distributed denial-of-service (DDoS) attacks.

- **Unauthorized Access to Player Accounts:** Weak passwords and lack of two-factor authentication (2FA) can lead to compromised accounts.

- **Fake Browser Games or Clones:** Fraudulent games mimic popular titles to deceive players.

- **Lack of Parental Controls:** Children playing browser games may inadvertently access inappropriate content or fall victim to scams.

PC Games

PC games are video games played on personal computers (PCs) rather than on dedicated gaming consoles or mobile devices. They leverage the capabilities of a PC's hardware and software, providing gamers with versatile and customizable experiences. PC games are distributed through physical media, digital downloads, or online platforms and cater to a wide range of genres and audiences.

PC games run mostly on the following personal computers platforms:

- Windows

- macOS

- Linux

General PC game features include the following:

- Offers the most diverse range of games, from indie titles to AAA releases

- Distributed via digital platforms like Steam, Epic Games Store, and GOG, or downloaded directly from developers

- Often supports mods for customization or enhanced gameplay

Here are some key characteristics of PC games:

- **Customizability:** Players can adjust graphics, controls, and other game settings to suit their hardware and preferences.

- **Wide Variety of Input Devices:** PC games support various input methods, including keyboards, mice, game controllers, and VR devices.

- **Diverse Game Library:** PC games span virtually every genre, from first-person shooters (FPS) and role-playing games (RPGs) to simulation and puzzle games.

- **Superior Graphics and Performance:** PCs with high-end hardware can deliver better graphics, higher resolutions, and faster frame rates compared to consoles or mobile devices.

- **Online Ecosystems:** Digital distribution platforms like Steam, Epic Games Store, GOG, and Origin provide access to extensive game libraries, community features, and multiplayer matchmaking.

- **Backward Compatibility:** Many PC games, even older titles, can often be played on modern systems with minor adjustments or compatibility layers.

PC games include different player options like

1. **Single-Player Games:**
   - Designed for solo play, these games often feature rich narratives or challenging gameplay mechanics.

2. **Multiplayer Games:**

- Enable players to compete or cooperate with others online or on local networks.

3. **Massively Multiplayer Online Games (MMOs):**

- Large-scale games with persistent worlds where thousands of players interact simultaneously.

4. **Free-to-Play Games:**

- Games available for free, often monetized through microtransactions or cosmetic items.

5. **Indie Games:**

- Games developed by independent creators or small studios, often showcasing unique concepts or art styles.

PC gaming offers several benefits, ranging from superior hardware capabilities to customization options. These advantages make PC gaming an attractive choice for players who value performance, flexibility, and a wide variety of game options. PC gaming stands out for its flexibility, performance, and rich ecosystem, making it a favored platform for a wide range of gamers. While it requires an upfront investment and technical knowledge, its long-term benefits often outweigh the challenges.

PC gaming offers several benefits including

- **Flexibility**: PCs offer customizable settings for graphics, controls, and mods.

- **Performance**: High-end PCs deliver superior visuals and faster frame rates.

- **Game Variety**: A vast library of games, including indie and exclusive titles.

- **Backward Compatibility**: Ability to play older games with modern systems.

- **Community Features**: Strong modding communities and active online player bases.

There are of course also disadvantages of PC gaming that can affect accessibility, cost, and user experience.

While PC gaming offers unparalleled flexibility, performance, and variety, its disadvantages, such as high costs, complexity, and maintenance requirements, can be significant barriers. Gamers must weigh these factors against their preferences and needs to determine if PC gaming is the right choice for them.

Here are some of the main disadvantages of PC gaming:

- **Cost**: High-performance PCs can be expensive to build or purchase.

- **Complexity**: Maintaining hardware and troubleshooting issues require technical knowledge.

- **Hardware Upgrades**: Frequent upgrades may be necessary to play newer games at optimal settings.

- **Cheating**: Open platforms sometimes lead to increased instances of cheating in multiplayer games.

Based on Statista source, in 2024, the PC gaming landscape was dominated by several key genres that captivated players worldwide including

- **Shooter games**
- **Action-adventure games**
- **Role-playing games (RPGs)**
- **Battle royale games**

- **Strategy games**

- **Simulation games**

- **Sports games**

- **Puzzle and idle games**

Top ten popular PC games in 2024 were (source Newzoo)

1. **Roblox**

2. **Minecraft**

3. **Fortnite**

4. **Counter-Strike 2 and GO**

5. **Call of Duty: Modern Warfare II/III/Warzone 2.0**

6. **The Sims 4**

7. **League of Legends**

8. **Valorant**

9. **Grand Theft Auto V**

10. **Overwatch 1 and 2**

Cybersecurity Concerns in PC Games

Cybersecurity risks generally include

- Pirated versions of games containing malware

- Cheating tools or mods acting as Trojan horses

- Account hacking on popular distribution platforms

- Ransomware targeting gamers with valuable libraries

More specifically, PC game cybersecurity risks, which can compromise player data, devices, and even broader systems, include

- **Malware and Phishing:** Game cracks, cheats, or unofficial downloads often hide malware or lead to phishing attempts, compromising user data or injecting malicious code.

- **Account Takeovers:** Weak passwords or phishing attacks can lead to unauthorized access to gaming accounts, which may store personal information or payment details.

- **Distributed Denial-of-Service (DDoS) Attacks:** Players might be targeted by adversaries to disrupt their gaming experience or extort them for ransom.

- **In-Game Currency and Item Theft:** Hackers can exploit vulnerabilities to steal virtual goods or game currency, affecting gameplay and causing financial loss.

- **Identity Theft:** Personal information provided during account creation or transactions could be compromised, leading to identity theft or fraud.

- **Social Engineering:** Attackers may exploit trust or manipulate players into revealing sensitive information through social engineering tactics in online interactions or forums.

- **Game Mods and Third-Party Software:** Mods or third-party software can contain malware or vulnerabilities that compromise system security when installed alongside games.

Downloaded Games

Downloaded games are video games that are obtained and installed on a device (such as a PC, console, or mobile device) via the Internet, rather than being played from a physical disc or cartridge. These games are typically purchased or accessed through digital storefronts and platforms like

- Google Play Store

- App Store (iOS)

- Steam

- Epic Games Store

- PlayStation Store

- Xbox Store

- Nintendo eShop

Downloaded games, after being downloaded, are generally installed on various device platforms including

- PCs

- Consoles

- Mobile

General downloaded game features include the following:

- Available across multiple devices

- Offers offline play for many titles

- Generally provides better graphics and performance than browser-based games

Key characteristics of downloaded games include

- **Digital Format:** The game files are stored digitally on the device's storage, such as a hard drive or SSD.

- **Internet Connection:** Requires an Internet connection to download the game files.

- **No Physical Media:** Eliminates the need for physical discs or cartridges, making the process faster and more convenient.

- **Accessibility:** Once downloaded, the game is typically accessible anytime without needing to insert a disc.

- **Updates and Patches:** Downloaded games can be easily updated or patched by the developer over the Internet.

Major Benefits of Downloaded Games

Downloaded games provide convenience, instant access, cost savings, and environmental benefits, making them a popular choice for gamers worldwide.

Benefits of downloaded games might include

- **Convenience and Accessibility:** Games can be purchased and downloaded instantly from online stores without leaving home. There are no need to handle or store physical discs or cartridges. Finally, players can access and play the games anytime, as long as they're installed on their device.

- **Faster Availability:** Digital games are available for download immediately upon release (or even predownloaded for early access), reducing wait times compared to purchasing physical copies.

- **Automatic Updates:** Game patches, updates, and expansions are automatically downloaded, ensuring the game remains up to date without manual effort.

- **Portability:** Games can be redownloaded on other compatible devices using the same account, making it easier to switch between systems or upgrade hardware.

- **Eco-Friendly:** Downloaded games reduce waste associated with manufacturing, packaging, and shipping physical copies.

- **Often Cheaper Deals:** Digital storefronts frequently offer discounts, bundle deals, or seasonal sales (e.g., Steam Summer Sale), making games more affordable than physical editions.

Based on Statista source, in 2024, the most downloaded genres like action, RPGs, battle royale, and sports offered immersive and accessible experiences for diverse player preferences.

The most prevalent downloaded game genres in 2024 were (source Statista)

- **Action games**
- **Role-playing games (RPGs)**
- **Battle royale**
- **Sports and racing games**
- **Adventure games**

- **Simulation games**

- **Survival and horror**

- **Multiplayer online battle arena (MOBA)**

- **Puzzle and casual games**

- **First-person and third-person shooters**

- **Strategy games**

- **MMORPGs (massively multiplayer online role-playing games)**

The top ten downloaded games in 2024 were (source Newzoo)

1. **Roblox**

2. **Block Blast!**

3. **Subway Surfers**

4. **Pizza Ready!**

5. **Ludo King**

6. **Free Fire: Winterlands**

7. **Free Fire MAX**

8. **Offline Games**

9. **Ball Pool**

10. **My Talking Tom 2**

Cybersecurity Concerns in Downloaded Games

Cybersecurity risks generally include

- Malware embedded in unofficial downloads

- Fake websites distributing illegitimate game files

- Exploits in outdated or unpatched game versions

More specifically, downloaded game cybersecurity risks, which can compromise player data, devices, and even broader systems, include

- **Malware and Viruses:** Downloading games from untrusted sources, torrent sites, or unofficial platforms can result in malware, ransomware, or viruses being bundled with the game files.

- **Phishing Attacks:** Gamers may be tricked into clicking fake download links, logging into fake platforms, or providing sensitive information on phishing sites.

- **Insecure Platforms:** Downloading games from poorly secured or illegitimate online platforms may expose users to attacks.

- **Compromised Game Mods or Cheats:** Mods, cheats, or patches downloaded from unofficial sources may include hidden malicious code.

- **Weak Account Security:** Using weak passwords, not enabling two-factor authentication (2FA), or reusing credentials across platforms increases the risk of account breaches.

- **Data Harvesting:** Some games or platforms may collect excessive personal data or track user behavior without proper consent.

- **Pirated or Cracked Games:** Illegally downloaded games often contain embedded malware or adware and lack proper updates or security patches.

- **Man-in-the-Middle Attacks (MITM):** Unsecured Wi-Fi networks can allow attackers to intercept data during downloads or online gameplay sessions.

- **Social Engineering and Chat Scams:** Attackers may manipulate players through in-game chats, forums, or social platforms, tricking them into sharing sensitive information or downloading malicious files.

- **Exploitation of In-Game Purchases:** Hackers may exploit payment systems for in-game purchases or steal saved payment details.

Mobile Games

Mobile gaming refers to any type of video game that can be played on mobile devices, including smartphones and tablets. With the rise of mobile technology, games have become more advanced, offering experiences that range from simple puzzle games to complex role-playing games. Thanks to their accessibility and portability, mobile games have become one of the most popular forms of entertainment worldwide.

The history of mobile gaming began with early games like *Snake* on Nokia phones, which were simple, low-tech games. However, with advancements in mobile hardware, touchscreens, and powerful processors, mobile games have evolved into highly immersive and interactive experiences. Popular genres include action, strategy, puzzles, sports, and multiplayer games, offering something for everyone.

Mobile games are a rapidly growing segment of the gaming industry, designed to be played on smartphones and tablets. These games have become incredibly popular due to the widespread availability of mobile devices and the ease of access to app stores, where players can download games instantly.

Mobile games run on smartphones and tablets running Android or iOS platforms.

General mobile game features include the following:

- Casual and accessible, with a vast range of free-to-play games supported by in-app purchases

- Distribution via official app stores like Google Play and Apple's App Store

- Often integrated with social features like leaderboards or friends' lists

Key characteristics of mobile games include

- **Accessibility**: Mobile games can be played anywhere, anytime, making them incredibly convenient for short bursts of entertainment or longer gaming sessions.

- **Free-to-Play with In-App Purchases**: Many mobile games are free to download but include in-app purchases or ads, allowing developers to monetize the games while keeping them accessible.

- **Social Features**: Many mobile games include multiplayer modes, social features, or integration with platforms like Facebook, allowing players to connect with friends and share achievements.

- **Wide Range of Genres**: From casual, easy-to-play games like *Candy Crush* to action-packed games like *PUBG Mobile* and even strategy games like *Clash of Clans*, mobile games cater to a wide variety of tastes and preferences.

- **Regular Updates**: Mobile games often receive regular updates, adding new levels, characters, or features to keep players engaged and returning.

Based on Statista source, in 2024, mobile game genres like action, RPGs, battle royale, and sports offered the most immersive and accessible experiences for diverse player preferences.

The most prevalent mobile game genres in 2024 were (source Statista)

- **Puzzle games**

- **Action games**

- **Strategy games**

- **Casino games**

- **Role-playing games (RPGs)**

- **Hyper-casual games**

The top ten mobile games in 2024 were (source Newzoo)

1. **Roblox**

2. **Monopoly Go!**

3. **Twisted Tangle**

4. **Royal Match**

5. **Wood Nuts & Bolts Puzzle**

6. **Block Blast!**

7. **Help Me: Tricky Story**

8. **Traffic Escape!**

9. **Dice Dreams**

10. **Last War: Survival Game**

Cybersecurity Concerns in Mobile Games

Cybersecurity risks generally include

- Malware-laden apps on unofficial marketplaces

- Data theft due to poorly secured apps or permissions

- Phishing scams through in-game chats or ads

- Exploitation of microtransactions and unauthorized in-app purchases

More specifically, mobile game cybersecurity risks, which can compromise player data, devices, and even broader systems, include

As we saw, each type caters to different preferences and contexts, ensuring gamers have a wide variety of experiences to choose from. A summary of game key differences is shown in Table 1-1.

Table 1-1. *Game key differences*

Aspect	Console Games	Browser Games	PC Games	Downloaded Games	Mobile Games
Platform	Consoles	Web browsers	PCs	Multiple devices	Mobile devices
Hardware	Dedicated hardware	Minimal	Varies widely	Device-dependent	Smartphone/tablet
Graphics	High-quality	Simple	Highly customizable	Device-specific	Ranges from basic to advanced
Cost	Premium-priced	Often free	Varies widely	Varies	Free or in-app purchases
Gameplay Style	Immersive	Casual	Diverse	Broad range	Portable and accessible

Summary

In this chapter, we introduced why cybersecurity is such a critical concern in the gaming industry due to the significant financial investments, personal data, intellectual property, and many other reasons.

We then described shortly the different types of games in the market and how to protect player data and maintain a secure gaming environment in the gaming industry. Finally, we reminded how players and game developers must be trained and be vigilant to potential cybersecurity threats and what are the most important cybersecurity best practices in the gaming industry.

All gaming cybersecurity risks and impacts will be described in more detail in the upcoming chapters of this book.

CHAPTER 2

Key Aspects of Cybersecurity in the Gaming Industry

The gaming industry has become one of the largest and most lucrative sectors in the digital economy, with millions of players engaging in online multiplayer games, streaming services, and in-game purchases daily. As the industry continues to grow, it also faces an increasing array of cybersecurity challenges. From data breaches and ransomware attacks to cheating and account takeovers, the threats to gaming platforms, players, and developers are significant and evolving.

The gaming industry's cybersecurity challenges are multifaceted, spanning data protection, payment security, and safeguarding the overall gaming experience. Proactive measures, robust security policies, and continuous monitoring are essential to mitigating risks and building trust with players.

The gaming industry is a lucrative target for cybercriminals due to its massive user base, valuable digital assets, and sensitive user data.

In this chapter, we will focus on the key aspects of cybersecurity in the gaming industry in order to understand the risks and impacts involved for both players and game providers.

© Massimo Nardone 2025
M. Nardone, *Cybersecurity Threats and Attacks in the Gaming Industry*, Apress Pocket Guides,
https://doi.org/10.1007/979-8-8688-1492-1_2

Why Cybersecurity Matters in the Gaming Industry?

Cybersecurity in gaming is essential for maintaining trust among players, protecting investments, and ensuring a safe and enjoyable gaming environment.

Listed here are the major reasons why cybersecurity matters in the gaming industry:

- **Massive User Base:**
  Online gaming platforms host millions of players globally, collecting vast amounts of personal information, including names, email addresses, and payment details. These data sets are prime targets for cybercriminals.

- **High Revenue Potential:**
  With the rise of microtransactions, subscription services, and esports, the gaming industry generates billions of dollars annually. This financial aspect makes it a tempting target for attackers seeking to exploit vulnerabilities for monetary gain.

- **Complex Ecosystem:**
  Gaming involves diverse stakeholders, including developers, publishers, platforms, and players. Each layer of this ecosystem introduces potential vulnerabilities, from server-side exploits to client-side hacks.

- **Reputation and Trust:**
  For gaming companies, maintaining a secure
  environment is crucial for user trust. A single data
  breach or hacking incident can damage a company's
  reputation and lead to player attrition.

What Needs to Be Secured in the Gaming Industry and Why?

The gaming industry is a complex ecosystem involving developers, players, platforms, and networks. The need to secure various aspects of this ecosystem stems from the potential for financial, reputational, and operational harm caused by cyberattacks, cheating, and data breaches. Below is a breakdown of critical areas that require robust security measures and the reasons why they need protection.

When it comes to cybersecurity in the gaming industry, we must secure the following:

1. **Protecting Player Data**: Games often collect personal information and payment details. Cybersecurity ensures this data is protected from theft or misuse.

2. **Preventing Cheating**: Cheating can ruin the gaming experience and affect game economies. Robust cybersecurity measures help detect and prevent cheating.

3. **Maintaining Game Integrity**: Secure systems prevent unauthorized access, ensuring that game content, updates, and user interactions remain intact and reliable.

4. **Securing Transactions**: Many games involve in-game purchases or trading virtual goods. Cybersecurity safeguards these transactions from fraud and ensures fair play.

5. **Protecting Intellectual Property**: Game developers invest heavily in creating content. Cybersecurity prevents unauthorized copying or distribution of game assets.

6. **Safeguarding Online Communities**: Multiplayer games rely on community interactions. Cybersecurity helps protect players from harassment, scams, or other malicious activities.

Understanding Cybersecurity Risks in the Gaming Industry

The gaming industry faces several significant cybersecurity risks which might have of course different impacts for both player and technical provider.

For game player, the cybersecurity risks might be as follows:

- **Account Theft and Identity Fraud:**

  - **Player Accounts**: Gamers' accounts often hold valuable data, including personal information, payment details, and rare in-game items, making them attractive targets for hackers.

  - **Phishing Attacks**: Scams designed to trick players into sharing login credentials or personal details.

- **Reputation Damage from Hacks**: Leaks of unfinished games, source code, or internal communications can damage a company's reputation and competitive advantage.

- **Cheating and Exploits**: Hackers create cheats, mods, or exploits to gain unfair advantages in games, compromising the integrity of gameplay and diminishing user experience.

- **In-Game Fraud**: Fraudulent transactions or scams in games with real-money economies or marketplaces for virtual items can lead to financial losses for players and developers.

- **Data Breaches**: Game companies often store large amounts of user data, making them attractive targets for breaches, which can expose personal information of millions of players.

- **Social Engineering**: Gaming communities and forums can be exploited to manipulate players or developers into revealing sensitive information.

Instead, technical providers' cybersecurity risks might involve

- **DDoS (Distributed Denial-of-Service) Attacks:** Game servers can be overwhelmed by DDoS attacks, causing outages and disruptions for players. This is particularly common during competitive events or new game launches.

- **Ransomware Attacks:** Game studios can be targeted with ransomware, locking them out of their own systems until a ransom is paid, potentially delaying game development or releases.

- **Malware in Game Mods or Downloads:** Malicious software can be embedded in unofficial mods, patches, or pirated versions of games, infecting players' devices.

- **Supply Chain Vulnerabilities:** Third-party tools or platforms used in game development or distribution (e.g., SDKs, APIs) can be exploited as attack vectors.

- **IoT and Connected Devices Risks:** With the rise of VR/ AR and connected devices, vulnerabilities in gaming hardware can lead to unauthorized access or data theft.

- **Cryptojacking:** Hackers can use games or gaming platforms to mine cryptocurrency on players' devices without their knowledge, leading to performance degradation and energy costs.

- **Targeting Esports:** High-stakes esports events and tournaments are vulnerable to attacks aimed at disrupting competitions or gaining illicit advantages.

In both player and gaming technical provider spaces, we must make sure we are able to mitigate these explained risks.

Gaming technical providers should always adopt and employ advanced **anti-cheat systems** and robust **authentication mechanisms** like multi-factor authentication (MFA), ensuring that they regularly update and patch game software and servers as well as monitoring constantly for unusual activity and conducting regular security audits.

Of course, an important element is also making sure technical providers do educate players and staff on safe online practices to reduce susceptibility to scams and phishing.

In the gaming industry, cybersecurity is crucial due to several key elements including

- **Protection of intellectual property**

- **Protection of user data**

- **Prevention of cheating and exploits**

- **Protection against distributed denial-of-service (DDoS) attacks**

- **Securing in-game transactions**

- **Securing game infrastructure**

- **Training and awareness**

Let's understand these cybersecurity key elements in the gaming industry in more detail.

Protection of Intellectual Property

The protection of intellectual property (IP) in the gaming industry is a critical issue due to the significant value of creative assets, technology, and branding. IP laws help safeguard the interests of game developers, publishers, and creators while fostering innovation. The main risk related to protection of IP is the piracy and reverse engineering of games which can lead to revenue losses and unauthorized distribution.

The remediation to this risk includes the following:

- Use obfuscation and encryption to protect game code and assets

- Watermark digital assets to trace unauthorized usage

- Monitor piracy platforms and issue takedown notices when necessary

Let's understand a bit more about the types of IP in games:

Copyright:

- **Covers**: Original creative works, such as game code, artwork, music, characters, storylines, and cutscenes

- **Protection**: Prevents unauthorized reproduction, distribution, or adaptation of these elements

- **Duration**: Usually the lifetime of the creator plus a certain number of years (e.g., 70 years in the United States)

Trademarks:

- **Covers**: Logos, brand names, slogans, and distinctive elements associated with a game

- **Protection**: Ensures consumers can distinguish between products and protects brand identity

- **Duration**: Renewable as long as the trademark is actively used in commerce

Patents:

- **Covers**: Innovative game mechanics, systems, or technologies (e.g., unique matchmaking algorithms or virtual reality systems)

- **Protection**: Grants exclusive rights to the patent holder to use the invention

- **Duration**: Typically 20 years from the filing date

Trade Secrets:

- **Covers**: Proprietary information, such as algorithms, game design documents, and marketing strategies

- **Protection**: Requires maintaining confidentiality and implementing safeguards

- **Duration**: Indefinite as long as the information remains secret

Protection of User Data

The gaming industry handles massive amounts of user data, including personal information, payment details, and behavioral data. Protecting this data is crucial to maintain user trust, comply with regulations, and prevent data breaches.

The main issue related to the protection of user data is that games often collect personal information, including names, emails, payment details, and even biometric data which are exposed and must be protected.

At a general level, protection of user data can be achieved by the following:

- Implement encryption for data storage and transmission

- Ensure compliance with data privacy regulations like GDPR, CCPA, or COPPA (for child-focused games)

- Conduct regular audits to identify and mitigate vulnerabilities

What kind of user data do games collect?

- **Personal Identifiable Information (PII):**

  - Names, email addresses, phone numbers, and physical addresses.

  - Payment details for in-game purchases.

- **Behavioral and Usage Data:**

    - Gaming habits, preferences, and interactions.

    - Data collected through cookies, tracking, or gameplay analytics.

- **Sensitive Data:**

    - For certain games, additional sensitive information, such as voice recordings (from chats) or biometric data, may be collected.

In general, gamers' accounts can be targeted for their virtual assets, payment details, or personal information; therefore, we must ensure that we

- Use robust authentication mechanisms, including multi-factor authentication (MFA)

- Educate users on creating strong passwords and recognizing phishing attempts

- Monitor for suspicious login activities

Protection Against Cheating and Exploits

Cheating and exploits can disrupt the gaming experience, harm the integrity of competitive games, and damage a game's reputation. Protecting against these issues is critical for maintaining a fair and enjoyable experience for all players. Main risk is that cheating tools and exploits harm the gaming experience and can introduce security risks.

At a general level, protection against cheating and exploits can be achieved by the following:

- Deploy anti-cheat software to detect and block unauthorized modifications

- Regularly update and patch vulnerabilities in game code

- Employ machine learning to identify abnormal behavior patterns indicative of cheating

Common cheating and exploit types include the following:

Cheating Tools and Hacks:

- **Aimbots**: Automated aiming assistance for shooters

- **Wall Hacks**: Allow players to see through walls or obstacles

- **Speed Hacks**: Increase a player's movement speed beyond normal limits

Exploits:

- **Glitches**: Using unintended bugs in the game for an unfair advantage (e.g., duplication glitches)

- **Economy Exploits**: Manipulating in-game economies for unfair gains

Social Engineering:

- **Account Theft**: Using phishing or scams to steal accounts

- **Match Fixing**: Colluding with other players to manipulate outcomes in ranked or competitive play

Botting and Automation:

- Automating repetitive tasks like resource gathering in MMORPGs

We need to understand the key strategies for anti-cheat protection that should be adopted in the gaming industry.

Here are some examples of key strategies:

Anti-cheat Software:

- Implement dedicated anti-cheat tools to detect and block cheating

- Examples:

  - **Easy Anti-cheat**: Used by games like *Apex Legends*

  - **BattlEye**: Used in games like *PUBG*

  - **Vanguard**: Developed by Riot Games for *Valorant*

Server-Side Validation:

- Use server-side processing to validate player actions and detect anomalies (e.g., impossible movements, excessive damage)

Encryption and Obfuscation:

- Encrypt game code and network traffic to make it harder for hackers to reverse engineer or intercept data

Behavioral Analysis:

- Use machine learning to identify unusual patterns in gameplay behavior that may indicate cheating

Player Reporting Systems:

- Allow players to report suspected cheaters, enabling manual reviews and data collection for automated detection

Hardware Bans:

- Ban the hardware IDs of devices used by repeat offenders to prevent them from easily creating new accounts

By combining robust technical measures, community involvement, and legal enforcement, the gaming industry can effectively combat cheating and exploits while fostering a fair and competitive environment for players.

Protection Against Distributed Denial-of-Service (DDoS) Attacks

We must secure game servers and networks, and in general, game servers are vulnerable to DDoS attacks, SQL injection, and other exploits.

The gaming industry is a prime target for distributed denial-of-service (DDoS) attacks, which can disrupt servers, affect gameplay, and damage a company's reputation. Protecting against these attacks is crucial to maintaining service availability and ensuring a seamless gaming experience.

When designing gaming servers and networks, we must make sure that we

- Use firewalls and intrusion detection/prevention systems (IDS/IPS) to safeguard servers

- Implement rate limiting and DDoS mitigation tools

- Regularly monitor and patch server vulnerabilities

What Is a DDoS attack?

A DDoS attack involves overwhelming a server, network, or service with an excessive amount of traffic, rendering it unavailable to legitimate users.

Types of DDoS attacks are

- **Volume-Based Attacks**: Flood servers with high traffic (e.g., UDP floods, ICMP floods)

- **Protocol Attacks**: Exploit weaknesses in network protocols (e.g., SYN floods, Ping of Death)

- **Application Layer Attacks**: Target specific services like login systems or game matchmaking

Advanced techniques for DDoS protection include the following:
AI and Machine Learning:

- Leverage AI to identify and block sophisticated DDoS attacks in real time

- Analyze traffic behavior and implement automated mitigation strategies

Edge Computing:

- Deploy resources at the network edge to absorb and process traffic locally, reducing the impact on core systems

Blockchain Technology:

- Use decentralized networks for secure, distributed hosting that makes it harder for attackers to disrupt services

By implementing robust preventive, mitigative, and responsive strategies, the gaming industry can effectively defend against DDoS attacks, ensuring smooth gameplay experiences and protecting its reputation.

In Chapter 4, we will describe in more detail how DDoS attacks work and how to defend against them.

Securing In-Game Transactions

In-game transactions, such as purchasing virtual goods, currency, or subscriptions, are a significant part of the gaming industry's revenue. However, they also pose security risks, including fraud, data breaches, and unauthorized transactions. Ensuring the security of in-game transactions is essential to protect players and maintain trust.

Key risks in in-game transactions include

- **Financial Fraud:**

    - Unauthorized use of payment methods, such as credit card fraud or stolen account credentials

- **Data Breaches:**

    - Exposure of sensitive user data, including payment details, personal information, and transaction history

- **Fake or Phishing Platforms:**

    - Fraudulent websites or apps posing as legitimate game platforms to steal payment information

- **Chargebacks and Refund Abuse:**

    - Users exploiting refund policies to retain purchased items while recovering their payment

- **Virtual Goods Theft:**

  - Hacking accounts to steal valuable in-game assets or currency

In-game transactions are an integral part of the gaming ecosystem, providing monetization opportunities for developers and enhancing gameplay experiences for players. However, securing these transactions is critical to protect users' sensitive information and maintain trust.

Below are comprehensive security measures that address the challenges and risks associated with in-game transactions:

- **Secure Payment Processing:**

  - **Encryption**

    1. Use end-to-end encryption (e.g., TLS/SSL) to protect payment data during transmission.

  - **Tokenization**

    1. Replace sensitive payment information with secure tokens to prevent unauthorized access.

  - **PCI DSS Compliance**

  - Adhere to Payment Card Industry Data Security Standards for secure handling of payment card data.

- **Multi-factor Authentication (MFA):**

  - Require MFA for user accounts to prevent unauthorized access and safeguard transactions.

- **Fraud Detection Systems:**

  - Implement machine learning models to monitor transactions for unusual patterns, such as

    1. Rapid purchases.

    2. Purchases from high-risk locations.

    3. Mismatched user behavior.

- **Secure APIs:**

  - Ensure APIs used for payment processing and transaction handling are secure against attacks like man-in-the-middle (MITM) or injection attacks.

- **Account Security Features:**

  - Features like login notifications, suspicious activity alerts, and mandatory strong passwords can help prevent account-related fraud.

Securing Game Infrastructure

The gaming industry has grown exponentially, driven by advancements in technology, the rise of multiplayer and online games, and an increasing number of players globally. This growth has made gaming platforms and infrastructure a prime target for cyberattacks, including data breaches, DDoS attacks, cheating, and exploitation. Securing game infrastructure is critical to ensuring a seamless gaming experience, protecting user data, and maintaining trust in the brand.

Game infrastructure encompasses the systems and technologies that power a gaming platform, including

- **Game Servers**: Host multiplayer sessions, manage matchmaking, and synchronize game states

- **Databases**: Store player data, game progress, and financial transactions

- **Networks**: Facilitate communication between players and servers

- **APIs**: Enable integrations with third-party services like payment gateways, analytics tools, or social platforms

- **Cloud Services**: Provide scalability and flexibility for hosting game assets and servers

Why Is Securing Game Infrastructure Important?

When designing game infrastructure, we must consider elements like how to secure user data, the payer experiences, etc.

Listed here are the most common reasons to secure game infrastructure:

1. **Player Experience**: Downtime or disruptions caused by cyberattacks can lead to a poor user experience and frustration among players.

2. **Data Protection**: Safeguarding player data, including personal information and financial details, is essential to comply with privacy laws and build trust.

3. **Revenue Protection**: Cheating, fraud, and service disruptions can lead to significant financial losses.

4. **Reputation Management**: A breach or attack can damage a game's reputation and lead to player attrition.

5. **Competitive Integrity**: Ensuring fair gameplay by preventing cheating and exploitation is crucial in fostering competitive environments, especially in esports.

The common threats to game infrastructure include

1. **DDoS Attacks**: Overloading servers to cause service outages

2. **Cheating and Exploits**: Manipulating game mechanics to gain an unfair advantage

3. **Data Breaches**: Unauthorized access to sensitive player or company data

4. **Account Hijacking**: Compromising user accounts through credential theft or phishing

5. **Ransomware Attacks**: Encrypting critical game infrastructure and demanding a ransom

6. **API Exploits**: Abusing insecure APIs to access or manipulate game services

In Chapter 4, the common threats to game infrastructure will be explained in more detail.

As securing game infrastructure is vital for protecting the integrity, functionality, and user experience of gaming platforms, we must understand the objectives that outline the primary goals of securing game infrastructure, which are as follows:

1. **Ensure Service Availability**: Protect servers from downtime or degradation caused by attacks

2. **Protect Data Integrity**: Safeguard user and game data from unauthorized access or tampering

3. **Maintain Fair Play**: Prevent exploits and cheating to uphold the integrity of the game

4. **Enable Scalability**: Implement security measures that support growth without compromising performance

5. **Comply with Regulations**: Adhere to data protection and cybersecurity laws, such as GDPR and CCPA

Training and Awareness in the Gaming Industry

As the gaming industry grows in scale and complexity, it faces increasing risks related to cybersecurity, privacy, and ethical gameplay. Training and awareness are essential for mitigating these risks and ensuring all stakeholders, including employees, players, and partners, understand their roles in maintaining a secure and ethical environment.

By investing in targeted education for employees, players, and partners, gaming companies can create a more secure, fair, and enjoyable ecosystem. Such efforts not only safeguard assets but also enhance user trust and long-term engagement.

The importance of training and awareness in gaming includes

1. **Cybersecurity Resilience**: Employees trained in cybersecurity best practices can better identify and respond to threats, reducing the risk of breaches.

2. **Compliance with Regulations**: Awareness of legal requirements (e.g., GDPR, COPPA) ensures adherence to data protection and privacy laws.

3. **Fair Play and Ethical Standards**: Educating players about acceptable behaviors promotes a fair and enjoyable gaming experience.

4. **Protecting Intellectual Property (IP)**: Employees and partners trained to safeguard proprietary information can prevent leaks and piracy.

5. **User Trust and Safety**: Players who understand security risks and how to protect themselves are less vulnerable to fraud, account theft, or phishing attacks.

For each gaming organization, we need to organize the training and awareness program based on different key elements and different user groups like employees, players, partners, and third-party developers.

Here are the key areas for training and awareness based on roles:

- **For Employees:**

  - **Cybersecurity Best Practices**: Training on password management, phishing awareness, and secure data handling

  - **Data Protection and Privacy Laws**: Familiarity with regulations like GDPR, CCPA, and COPPA

  - **Incident Response Protocols**: Steps to take in the event of a security breach or attack

  - **Anti-cheating Measures**: Understanding the tools and techniques used to detect and prevent cheating

  - **IP Protection**: Awareness of policies for handling proprietary game assets, code, and designs

- **For Players:**

  - **Account Security**: Importance of strong passwords, enabling multi-factor authentication (MFA), and avoiding sharing account details

- **Recognizing Scams**: Tips to identify phishing emails, fake websites, or fraudulent offers

- **Fair Play Guidelines**: Rules against cheating, exploiting bugs, or toxic behavior

- **Transaction Safety**: Safe practices for making in-game purchases and trading virtual assets

- **For Partners and Third-Party Developers:**

  - **Secure Development Practices**: Adhering to secure coding standards and avoiding vulnerabilities

  - **Contractual Obligations**: Compliance with security, privacy, and IP clauses in agreements

  - **Access Control**: Ensuring appropriate permissions and secure access to shared resources

The gaming industry employs a variety of training methods to enhance the skills of developers, designers, testers, and other professionals. These methods aim to keep the workforce updated with the latest technologies, trends, and practices while fostering creativity and collaboration.

Here are some prominent training methods used in the gaming industry:

1. **Interactive Workshops and Seminars:**

   - Conduct hands-on sessions for employees on secure coding practices, ethical gameplay monitoring, and incident response

2. **Online Courses and Certifications:**

   - Provide courses on cybersecurity fundamentals, privacy laws, or gaming-specific security tools (e.g., anti-cheat systems)

3. **Gamification:**

   - Use game-like elements to train employees or players on security topics, making the learning process engaging and memorable

4. **Simulated Cyberattacks:**

   - Run phishing simulations and penetration tests to train employees in recognizing and responding to real-world threats

5. **Community Engagement:**

   - Organize forums, webinars, or online events to educate players about fair play and online safety

6. **Documentation and Guides:**

   - Provide comprehensive resources, such as FAQs, user guides, or videos, that cover security, privacy, and gameplay ethics

Promoting awareness in the gaming ecosystem is essential to foster a healthy, inclusive, and innovative environment for players, developers, publishers, and other stakeholders. Raising awareness can address key challenges, educate users, and support the growth of the industry.

Below are strategies and approaches to promote awareness in the gaming ecosystem:

1. **Internal Communication:**

   - Regularly share updates, alerts, and best practices with employees through newsletters, meetings, or an intranet portal

2. **In-Game Messaging:**

- Use pop-ups, tutorials, or loading screen tips to educate players on account security, fair play, and transaction safety

3. **Social Media Campaigns:**

- Leverage social media platforms to spread awareness about safe gaming practices and upcoming security features

4. **Partnerships with Security Experts:**

- Collaborate with cybersecurity firms or organizations to develop training content and tools tailored to the gaming industry

5. **Incentivize Participation:**

- Reward employees or players who actively engage in training programs or contribute to promoting a secure gaming environment

Summary

In this chapter, we introduced why cybersecurity is such a critical concern in the gaming industry due to the significant financial investments, personal data, intellectual property, and many other reasons.

We then described shortly the different types of games in the market and how to protect player data and maintain a secure gaming environment in the gaming industry. Finally, we reminded how players and game developers must be trained and be vigilant to potential cybersecurity threats and what are the most important cybersecurity best practices in the gaming industry.

All gaming cybersecurity risks and impacts will be described in more detail in the upcoming chapters of this book.

CHAPTER 3

Games Targeted by Cybersecurity Attacks

Cybersecurity attacks can target a wide range of games and gaming platforms, often due to their popularity, in-game economies, and the sensitive data they handle.

In this chapter, we will focus on how, which, and why certain types of games are targets of cybersecurity attacks.

Here are some of the most common types of games and platforms that are frequently targeted and will be elaborated in this chapter:

- **Online multiplayer games**
- **Massively multiplayer online role-playing games (MMORPGs)**
- **Mobile games**
- **Games with in-game purchases or microtransactions**
- **Gaming platforms and marketplaces**

Let's explore some of them.

© Massimo Nardone 2025
M. Nardone, *Cybersecurity Threats and Attacks in the Gaming Industry*, Apress Pocket Guides, https://doi.org/10.1007/979-8-8688-1492-1_3

Online Multiplayer Games

Online multiplayer games are video games that allow multiple players to interact, compete, or cooperate over the Internet in a shared virtual environment. These games can range from casual experiences to competitive esports titles and massive open-world adventures.

- **Examples of Games:**
  - Fortnite
  - League of Legends
  - Call of Duty: Warzone, Apex Legends

Online multiplayer games are prime targets for cybersecurity attacks due to their vast user base, financial transactions, and in-game economies. Here are some of the reasons why cybercriminals target them:

- **Large user base and sensitive data**
- **Financial incentives and in-game economies**
- **Distributed denial-of-service (DDoS) attacks**
- **Cheating and exploits**
- **Social engineering and phishing**
- **Insider threats and developer exploits**

Let's understand better some of the above reasons.

- **Large User Base and Sensitive Data**

  Cybercriminals know that for large user base games, for instance, Call of Duty, there are millions of players that share personal information like emails, addresses, payment details, etc. Having access to these sensitive user information helps cybercriminals to customize cybersecurity attacks with methods like email phishing for instance.

Credential stuffing is a cyberattack where hackers use leaked username-password pairs from data breaches to gain unauthorized access to gaming accounts. Since many users reuse passwords across multiple platforms, attackers can exploit stolen credentials from one service to break into another—especially gaming accounts that store valuable in-game assets, personal information, and payment details.

Credential stuffing is very common since many users reuse passwords.

- **Financial Incentives and In-Game Economies**

  In-game economies and financial incentives play a crucial role in shaping player behavior, monetization strategies, and game longevity. Developers create economic systems that drive engagement, retention, and revenue, while players navigate these systems to earn, trade, or purchase virtual goods.

  In game economics, we must consider the following key components:

  Virtual Currencies:

  - Used to facilitate transactions within the game.
  - Examples:

- **Hard Currency**: Purchased with real money (e.g., V-Bucks in *Fortnite*).

- **Soft Currency**: Earned through gameplay (e.g., Gold in *World of Warcraft*).

In-Game Items and Assets:

- Virtual goods like skins, weapons, or upgrades that enhance gameplay or personalization.

- Some items have real-world value (e.g., rare skins in *CS:GO*).

Player-Driven Marketplaces:

- Some games allow peer-to-peer trading or sales, leading to emergent economies.

- Examples:

  - **Counter-Strike: Global Offensive (CS:GO)**: Skin trading with real-money value.

  - **Axie Infinity:** Play-to-earn model with NFT-based assets.

Loot Boxes and Gacha Mechanics:

- Randomized rewards that incentivize spending for rare items.

- Often criticized for resembling gambling.

Subscription Models and Battle Passes:

- Provide ongoing rewards for recurring payments.

- **Example:** *Fortnite Battle Pass* offers exclusive cosmetics and challenges.

- **Cheating and Exploits**

Cheating and exploits have long been a challenge in the gaming industry, affecting fair play, game integrity, and monetization. As online multiplayer and competitive gaming continue to grow, developers must constantly combat cheating methods that harm the player experience.

Here are some examples of the types of cheating in games:

Software-Based Cheats:
- Third-party programs modify game files or inject code to gain unfair advantages:

  - **Aimbots**: Automatically aim and shoot at enemies (common in FPS games like *Call of Duty* and *CS:GO*).

  - **Wallhacks**: Allow players to see through walls (used in shooters like *Valorant*).

  - **Speed Hacks**: Increase player movement speed beyond normal limits.

  - **ESP (Extra Sensory Perception)**: Shows enemy locations, health, and other hidden information.

Hardware Exploits:
- Physical devices or modifications used to cheat:

  - **Cronus Zen and XIM Adapters**: Bypass controller restrictions for aim assist abuse.

  - **Modified Consoles**: Jailbreaking or modding consoles to run cheat software.

Exploits and Glitches:

- Bugs in the game that players use for unfair advantage:

    - **Duplication Glitches**: Players duplicate items, currency, or resources (common in MMOs).

    - **Invincibility Glitches**: Bugs that make characters immune to damage.

    - **Clipping and Out-of-Bounds Exploits**: Players hide in unintended areas for unfair advantages.

Social Engineering and Account Cheating

- Manipulating systems or people for unfair gains:

    - **Account Sharing and Boosting**: Skilled players log into weaker players' accounts to level them up.

    - **Scamming**: Trick other players into giving up valuable items.

    - **DDoS (Distributed Denial-of-Service) Attacks**: Crashing game servers to disrupt matches.

Bots and Automation

- Automated scripts perform in-game actions without human input:

    - **Gold Farming Bots**: Automatically farm resources in MMOs to sell for real money.

    - **AFK Bots**: Bots that stay active in matches to farm XP without playing.

Cheating and exploits continue to be a major challenge in gaming, but developers are fighting back with advanced detection, legal action, and stricter security measures. Balancing fair play with privacy and player experience will shape the future of anti-cheat efforts.

With the rise of blockchain gaming, esports, and cloud gaming, the cybersecurity threats will continue to evolve, making protection measures even more crucial. To stay safe while playing online multiplayer games, it is best practice to

- **Use strong, unique passwords and enable 2FA (two-factor authentication)**

- **Avoid third-party mods or cheats—they often contain malware**

- **Watch out for phishing links in chats, emails, or fake game sites**

- **Keep software and games updated to patch security vulnerabilities**

Let's analyze now the massively multiplayer online role-playing games (MMORPGs).

Massively Multiplayer Online Role-Playing Games (MMORPGs)

Massively multiplayer online role-playing games (MMORPGs) are one of the most immersive and socially driven genres in the gaming industry. These games feature vast virtual worlds where players interact, complete quests, level up characters, and engage in large-scale battles. MMORPGs have evolved significantly since their early days, with modern games incorporating innovative monetization, gameplay mechanics, and community-driven content.

- **Examples of Games:**
  - **World of Warcraft**
  - **Final Fantasy XIV**
  - **Elder Scrolls**

Online multiplayer games are prime targets for cybersecurity attacks because they often have complex in-game economies and valuable virtual items, which can be sold for real money. Hackers may target accounts to steal these assets.

The key features of MMORPGs include the following:

- **Persistent Online Worlds:**
  - MMORPGs run on servers that allow players to interact in real time.
  - Worlds continue evolving even when a player is offline.

- **Character Progression and Customization:**
  - Players develop characters through experience points (XP), skills, and equipment.
  - Extensive customization includes races, classes, abilities, and cosmetic options.

- **Open-Ended Gameplay:**
  - Players choose how they engage with the game: PvE (player vs. environment), PvP (player vs. player), or social activities.

- **Player-Driven Economies:**

  - MMORPGs often feature in-game marketplaces where players trade items, weapons, and currency.

  - Some economies extend into real-world trading (*RuneScape, World of Warcraft* gold-selling).

- **Social and Guild Systems:**

  - Players form guilds, parties, or alliances to tackle high-level content.

  - Community-driven content (events, raids, in-game politics) enhances immersion.

MMORPGs have evolved significantly over the past few decades, shaping the gaming industry with persistent worlds, social interactions, and expansive gameplay mechanics. Below is a historical timeline of their development:

A. **Classic Era (1990s–Early 2000s):**

  - **Ultima Online (1997):** One of the first MMORPGs with a persistent world

  - **EverQuest (1999):** Introduced large-scale raids and party-based gameplay

  - **RuneScape (2001):** Browser-based MMORPG with a massive economy

B. **Peak Popularity and WoW Era (2004–2010s):**

  - **World of Warcraft (2004):** Set industry standards with streamlined questing, PvP, and raids

  - **Guild Wars (2005):** Focused on PvP and nonsubscription model.

- **The Elder Scrolls Online (2014):** Brought a major single-player RPG franchise into the MMORPG space

C. **Modern and Hybrid MMORPGs (2010s–Present):**

- **Final Fantasy XIV (2013, Relaunch in 2014):** Resurged as one of the top MMORPGs with deep storytelling

- **Lost Ark (2022):** Mixed MMO elements with action RPG mechanics

- **New World (2021):** Brought open-world exploration with large-scale faction wars

The MMORPG industry faces numerous challenges, from technical hurdles to shifting player expectations.

Here are the most important of them:

Retaining Player Engagement:

- MMORPGs require **constant content updates** (new quests, expansions, raids) to keep players engaged.

- Games without fresh updates see player drop-offs (*WildStar, Star Wars: The Old Republic* struggled with this).

Balancing Monetization Without Pay-to-Win:

- Players expect fair monetization without feeling forced to spend money to compete.

- Some games lose player trust due to aggressive microtransactions (*Lineage 2M*).

Technical and Server Challenges:

- Large-scale MMORPGs need **strong server infrastructure** to handle thousands of simultaneous players.

- **DDoS attacks and server overloads** can cripple launches (*New World* faced issues).

Competing with Other Genres:

- Battle royales and live service games have attracted MMORPG players away.

- Developers now mix MMO elements into other genres (*Destiny 2, Genshin Impact*).

The MMORPG genre has evolved significantly, but it faces new challenges and opportunities as gaming technology and player expectations change.

Here's what the future may hold for MMORPGs:

- **Metaverse and VR Integration:** MMORPGs could evolve into persistent virtual worlds with deeper immersion.

- **AI-Driven NPCs and Dynamic Events:** AI could enable **procedural storytelling and evolving world events**.

- **Blockchain and Player-Owned Economies:** Some games explore **NFTs and play-to-earn models**, though controversial.

- **Cross-platform MMORPGs:** More games bridging PC, console, and mobile experiences.

MMORPGs remain one of the most engaging and socially immersive gaming genres, evolving to fit modern player expectations. With innovations in AI, monetization, and world building, the future of MMORPGs will likely continue blending persistent virtual worlds with new gaming trends.

Let's describe the key elements and challenges of mobile games.

Mobile Games

A mobile game is a video game designed to be played on smartphones, tablets, and other mobile devices. These games are typically optimized for touchscreen controls and can range from simple puzzle games to complex multiplayer experiences.

Mobile games are a prime target for cyberattacks due to their popularity, in-game purchases, and vast player bases.

- **Examples of Games:**
  - **Pokémon GO**
  - **Clash of Clans**
  - **Genshin Impact**

Mobile games are often targeted due to the ease of distributing malware through unofficial app stores or phishing scams. Players may also store payment information on their devices.

A successful mobile game balances engaging gameplay, smooth controls, social features, monetization, and performance optimization. The best games keep players coming back through rewards, updates, and immersive experiences.

Mobile games have evolved significantly, offering immersive experiences across various genres.

Below are some key features that make a mobile game engaging and successful:

- **Intuitive and Touch-Friendly Controls**

  - **Simple tap, swipe, drag, or tilt-based mechanics** for easy interaction

  - Optimized **UI/UX** to ensure smooth gameplay on different screen sizes

  - **Haptic feedback** and vibrations for better immersion

- **Engaging Gameplay and Mechanics**

  - **Casual or complex gameplay loops** to cater to different player types

  - **Levels, challenges, or open-world exploration** for variety

  - **Adaptive AI and difficulty scaling** to keep players engaged

- **Stunning Graphics and Animations**

  - **2D or 3D visuals** optimized for mobile devices

  - **Smooth animations** for realistic character movement

  - **VFX (visual effects)** like explosions, particle effects, and dynamic lighting

- **Multiplayer and Social Features**

  - **Real-time or turn-based multiplayer** (PvP or co-op modes)

  - **Leaderboards, achievements, and rankings** for competition

  - **In-game chat and friend invites** for social interaction

- **Monetization Strategies**

  - **In-App Purchases (IAPs):** Skins, characters, power-ups, etc.

  - **Rewarded Ads:** Watch ads to earn in-game currency or bonuses

  - **Subscription Models:** VIP access, exclusive content, or ad-free versions

- **Cross-platform and Cloud Syncing**

  - **Google Play/Apple Game Center integration** for cloud saves

  - **Cross-platform play** between mobile, PC, or consoles

  - **Seamless login with social media accounts** (Facebook, Google, Apple)

- **Regular Updates and Events**

  - **Seasonal updates** (new characters, skins, levels, or events)

  - **Limited-time challenges** to retain players

- **Bug fixes and performance optimizations** for smooth gameplay

- **Offline and Online Modes**

  - **Offline playability** for users with limited Internet access

  - **Online multiplayer and cloud syncing** for real-time interaction

  - **Autosave features** to prevent data loss

- **Adaptive Sound and Music**

  - **Dynamic soundtracks** that change based on gameplay

  - **Immersive sound effects (SFX)** like footsteps, gunfire, and environment sounds

  - **Customizable audio settings** for player preferences

- **AI and Personalization Features**

  - **Smart AI enemies and NPCs** that react dynamically

  - **Procedural level generation** for endless gameplay

  - **Personalized recommendations and adaptive difficulty** for player retention

Mobile gaming has become a massive industry, but with its growth comes significant cybersecurity threats. Hackers target mobile games for financial gains, data theft, and cheating.

Below are the key cybersecurity challenges faced by mobile games:

Cheating and Game Manipulation:

- Hackers use **modded APKs, game cheats, and memory editors** to gain unfair advantages.

- Players exploit vulnerabilities to **increase currency, unlock premium items, or manipulate leaderboards**.

- **Aimbots, wallhacks, and auto-clickers** ruin multiplayer integrity.

In-App Purchase (IAP) Fraud:

- Hackers exploit **payment loopholes** to get in-game purchases for free.

- Fake or **hacked in-app purchase (IAP) receipts** trick servers into granting premium items.

- **Phishing attacks** steal legitimate accounts with high-value assets.

Data Privacy and User Information Theft:

- Mobile games collect **user data (emails, passwords, payment info, geolocation, etc.)**.

- **Data leaks** can expose millions of player accounts.

- **Third-party SDKs and ads** may introduce privacy vulnerabilities.

Account Hijacking and Credential Stuffing:

- Hackers use **stolen credentials** from data breaches to take over accounts.

- Weak passwords make accounts vulnerable to **brute force attacks**.

- **Phishing attacks** trick users into giving login details.

Distributed Denial-of-Service (DDoS) Attacks:

- Attackers **overload game servers** to cause crashes and disrupt gameplay.

- Multiplayer games are **high targets** for DDoS attacks to gain an unfair advantage.

Reverse Engineering and Code Injection:

- Hackers **decompile game APKs** to modify game logic.

- **Code injection tools** allow attackers to alter game memory and bypass security.

- **Tampered game clients** enable cheating or piracy.

Fake Apps and Malware Distribution:

- Fake versions of popular games **infect devices with malware**.

- Rogue apps steal **player credentials, payment info, or device data**.

API and Server Exploits:

- Unsecured APIs allow attackers to **manipulate game data**.

- Poor server security exposes **leaderboards, matchmaking, and transactions**.

Ransomware and In-Game Extortion:

- Hackers **encrypt game data** and demand ransom for release.

- Some attackers **lock users out of their own accounts** for ransom.

Social Engineering and Scams:

- **Fake giveaways, free currency offers, and phishing links** steal accounts.

- Scammers impersonate **official game support** to trick players.

Cybersecurity is critical in mobile gaming to protect users, game integrity, and revenue. Implementing strong encryption, multi-factor authentication, anti-cheat measures, and API security can help reduce risks.

Games with In-Game Purchases or Microtransactions

Microtransactions have become a major revenue model for mobile, PC, and console games. These transactions allow players to buy in-game items, cosmetics, or upgrades using real money.

Games with microtransactions are targeted because they are lucrative targets for stealing payment information or exploiting vulnerabilities to obtain in-game currency or items.

Types of microtransactions in games include

- **Cosmetic Purchases:** Skins, emotes, outfits (e.g., Fortnite, Valorant)

- **Loot Boxes/Gacha:** Randomized rewards (e.g., Genshin Impact, FIFA Ultimate Team)

- **Battle Passes:** Tiered rewards over time (e.g., PUBG Mobile, Apex Legends)

- **Pay-to-Win Mechanics:** Buying stronger items (e.g., some mobile RPGs)

- **Speed Boosters:** Shortening upgrade times (e.g., Clash of Clans)

PC and console games with microtransactions include

- **Fortnite**

- **FIFA Series (Ultimate Team Mode)**

- **Grand Theft Auto Online (GTA Online)**

- **Apex Legends**

- **Call of Duty: Warzone/Modern Warfare**

- **Valorant**

- **League of Legends**

- **Overwatch 2**

- **The Elder Scrolls Online**

Examples of games include

- **PUBG Mobile**

- **Genshin Impact**

- **Clash of Clans/Clash Royale**

- **Call of Duty Mobile**

- **Candy Crush Saga**

- **Pokémon GO**

- **Free Fire**

- **Roblox**

- **Fortnite (mobile and console)**

Microtransactions are a major revenue source in modern gaming, offering in-game purchases for cosmetic items, upgrades, and more.

Games with in-game purchases or microtransaction key elements include the following:

Virtual Currency:

- Many games use an **in-game currency (e.g., V-Bucks, Apex Coins, Gems, Robux)** instead of direct cash payments.

- Encourages spending by making purchases feel less tangible.

Cosmetic Items and Skins:

- Nonessential but desirable items like **character skins, outfits, weapon skins, and emotes**.

- Common in **free-to-play games** (e.g., Fortnite, Valorant, Call of Duty Mobile).

Loot Boxes and Gacha Mechanics:

- Players **pay for randomized rewards** without knowing what they'll get.

- Often used in **Gacha games (e.g., Genshin Impact, FIFA Ultimate Team, Apex Legends)**.

- Criticized for promoting **gambling-like behavior**.

Battle Pass and Seasonal Rewards:

- **Tiered reward system** where players unlock items over time.

- Encourages **daily engagement and long-term spending**.

- Popular in games like **PUBG Mobile, Call of Duty, and Fortnite**.

Pay-to-Win Elements:

- Some games offer **gameplay advantages** in exchange for real money.

- Includes **stronger weapons, power-ups, and faster progress**.

- Controversial in competitive games as it gives paying users an unfair edge.

Limited-Time and Exclusive Offers:

- Creates a **sense of urgency** to buy items before they disappear.

- Used in events, holiday specials, or **rotating shop items**.

Subscription Models:

- Monthly or yearly **VIP programs** offering exclusive rewards.

- Common in games like **Clash Royale, Pokémon GO, and Roblox**.

Ads and Rewarded Videos:

- Some free games allow players to **watch ads for in-game rewards**.

- Used to **monetize nonpaying users** while still keeping engagement.

Microtransactions have reshaped gaming, offering both fair monetization models (cosmetics, battle passes) and controversial practices (loot boxes, pay-to-win features). Developers balance player experience and revenue generation, but some exploit these systems for maximum profit.

Let's have a look now at the challenges of games with in-game purchases (microtransactions).

Microtransactions have become a major part of gaming, but they also come with significant **challenges and controversies** for both players and developers. Here are the key issues:

Pay-to-Win (P2W) Mechanics:

- Some games allow **paying players to gain an unfair advantage** with better weapons, faster progression, or exclusive power-ups.

- **Example:** Some mobile RPGs and multiplayer shooters offer **premium gear that outclasses free items**.

Impact: Creates an unfair playing field, discouraging nonpaying players.

Loot Boxes and Gambling Concerns:

- Many games use **randomized loot boxes or gacha systems**, encouraging players to spend money for a *chance* at rare items.

- **Example:** FIFA Ultimate Team, Genshin Impact, and Apex Legends.

Impact: Can lead to **addictive spending** and even gambling-like behavior. Some countries have **banned loot boxes**.

High Costs and Predatory Pricing:

- Some games **overprice** digital items, leading to **unfair monetization**.

- **Example:** Fortnite and Call of Duty offer skins that can cost **$20-$100** each.

Impact: Players may feel pressured to spend **large sums** for exclusive content.

Limited-Time and FOMO Tactics:

- Developers use **time-limited offers and exclusive deals** to pressure players into spending quickly.

- **Example:** Seasonal skins in Overwatch 2 or timed battle pass rewards in Fortnite.

Impact: Triggers **impulse purchases** and **fear of missing out (FOMO)** tactics.

Account Theft and Fraud:

- In-game purchases make accounts valuable targets for **hackers and scammers**.

- **Example:** Fortnite, PUBG Mobile, and Roblox accounts are frequently hacked and resold.

Impact: Players risk losing money and progress if their accounts are stolen.

Monetization over Gameplay:

- Some games prioritize **microtransactions over fun and fair gameplay**.

- **Example:** Mobile games that **force long grind times** unless players pay for progress boosts.

Impact: Creates **frustration and paywalls** that harm player enjoyment.

Child Spending and Lack of Parental Controls:

- Many kids unknowingly **spend real money** on in-game purchases without parental permission.

- **Example:** Reports of children spending **hundreds or thousands of dollars** in mobile and console games.

Impact: Parents face **unexpected bills** and companies receive backlash for **poor spending controls**.

Regulatory and Legal Issues:

- Many governments are introducing **laws against exploitative microtransactions**.

- **Example:** Belgium and the Netherlands banned **loot boxes** in certain games.

Impact: Developers must **adapt monetization strategies** or face legal consequences.

While microtransactions help games generate revenue, they also pose **ethical, financial, and regulatory challenges**. Striking a **balance between fair monetization and player satisfaction** is key.

Gaming Platforms and Marketplaces

Gaming platforms and marketplaces provide players with access to games, in-game purchases, and social experiences. These platforms vary from PC, console, mobile, and cloud gaming services to online marketplaces for buying and selling games.

Let's have a look at the most used gaming platforms on the market:

PC Gaming Platforms:

- **Steam:** Largest PC gaming marketplace with thousands of titles

- **Epic Games Store:** Offers exclusive games and free weekly titles

- **GOG (Good Old Games):** DRM-free games with classic and modern releases

- **Microsoft Store:** Includes Xbox Game Pass for PC gaming

- **Itch.io:** Indie-friendly platform for small and experimental games

Console Gaming Platforms:

- **PlayStation Network (PSN):** Digital store for PlayStation games

- **Xbox Live/Microsoft Store:** Xbox games, Game Pass access

- **Nintendo eShop:** Digital store for Switch, 3DS, and Wii U games

- **PlayStation Now/Xbox Game Pass:** Subscription-based game libraries

Mobile Gaming Platforms:

- **Apple App Store:** iOS games and microtransaction-based titles

- **Google Play Store:** Android games, including free and paid games

- **Samsung Galaxy Store:** Alternative store for Samsung devices

Cloud Gaming Platforms:

- **Xbox Cloud Gaming (xCloud):** Play Xbox games via the cloud

- **NVIDIA GeForce Now:** Streams PC games from digital stores

- **PlayStation Plus Premium (Cloud Streaming):** Play older PlayStation titles online

- **Amazon Luna:** Subscription-based cloud gaming service

- **Boosteroid/Shadow PC:** Cloud PC gaming with various libraries

Gaming platforms and marketplaces face multiple challenges that impact players, developers, and publishers. These range from security risks and monopolistic control to fraudulent activities and ethical concerns.

Challenges in gaming platforms and marketplaces include the following:

Platform Monopolies and Revenue Cuts:

- Major platforms (Steam, PlayStation Store, Xbox Store, Apple App Store, Google Play) **take 30% revenue cuts** from developers.

- Smaller developers struggle with **high fees and limited profit margins**.

- Epic Games sued Apple and Google over **anti-competitive practices** (Fortnite lawsuit).

Impact: Less competition, higher game prices, and fewer earnings for developers.

Digital Rights Management (DRM) and Game Ownership:

- Many platforms **restrict game ownership** with DRM, requiring **online verification** (e.g., Denuvo).

- Players **don't truly "own" digital games** and risk losing access if platforms shut down.

- DRM can lead to **performance issues and piracy workarounds**.

Impact: Players have less control, and DRM can negatively affect game performance.

Fraudulent Game Keys and Scams:

- Key resellers (G2A, Kinguin) sometimes **sell stolen or fraudulent game keys**.

- Developers lose revenue when keys are bought with **stolen credit cards** and then refunded.

- Some platforms lack **proper buyer protection**, leading to scams.

Impact: Developers lose money, and players risk **buying revoked keys**.

Security Issues and Account Theft:

- Platforms face **account hacks, phishing, and credential stuffing attacks**.

- Steam, Epic Games, and PlayStation users frequently report **stolen accounts** due to weak security.

- Some marketplaces lack **two-factor authentication (2FA) or proper fraud prevention**.

Impact: Players lose valuable game libraries and in-game items.

In-Game Microtransactions and Loot Boxes:

- Marketplaces promote **loot boxes and microtransactions**, encouraging spending.

- Some games (FIFA, Genshin Impact, Call of Duty) rely on **gambling-like monetization**.

- Regulatory scrutiny is increasing, with **some countries banning loot boxes**.

Impact: Ethical concerns, gambling addiction, and unfair monetization practices.

Cross-platform Compatibility and Restrictions:

- Some games and services **lock content to specific platforms**, preventing cross-play.

- PlayStation historically restricted **cross-play with Xbox and PC** (e.g., Fortnite, Minecraft).

- Marketplace exclusivity deals **force players to buy from specific stores** (e.g., Epic vs. Steam).

Impact: Limits player choice and forces fragmented game libraries.

Cloud Gaming and Internet Dependence:

- Cloud gaming platforms (xCloud, GeForce Now, Amazon Luna) **require high-speed Internet**.

- Latency issues make cloud gaming **unplayable for users with weak connections**.

- Game ownership is at risk since **cloud services can shut down anytime** (e.g., Google Stadia).

Impact: Limits accessibility for players in regions with poor Internet infrastructure.

Toxicity and Content Moderation:

- Online gaming platforms (Xbox Live, PlayStation Network, Steam) **struggle with toxicity, hate speech, and cheating**.

- Some marketplaces lack **proper review systems**, leading to **fake or manipulated reviews**.

- Scalpers use bots to **hoard limited games and resell at inflated prices**.

Impact: Creates **unfair markets, misinformation, and hostile gaming communities**.

Gaming platforms and marketplaces are essential but face major challenges related to monopolies, security, fraud, and unfair monetization. Regulations, better security, and fairer revenue models are needed to improve the ecosystem.

Summary

In this chapter, we focus on how, which, and why certain types of games and platforms are frequently targeted.

We introduced the most common game platforms that are frequently targeted. All gaming cybersecurity risks and impacts will be described more in detail in the upcoming chapter of this book.

Finally, we defined how to protect games from cybersecurity attacks by following best practices so that both players and developers can reduce the risk of falling victim to cybersecurity attacks.

CHAPTER 4

Most common gaming Cybersecurity Attacks

The gaming industry, particularly the online gaming sector, is a prime target for various cybersecurity threats and attacks. This is due to the massive player base, the value of in-game items and currencies, the use of online infrastructure for multiplayer experiences, its large user base, valuable in-game assets, and vast online infrastructure.

Threats range from account takeovers to large-scale data breaches, impacting both players and gaming companies.

Cybersecurity threats in the gaming industry are evolving, targeting both players and game developers. As online gaming continues to grow, implementing robust security measures is crucial to protect user data, maintain fair gameplay, and ensure a safe gaming environment.

Cybersecurity **threats** and **attacks** are closely related but distinct concepts in cybersecurity.

© Massimo Nardone 2025
M. Nardone, *Cybersecurity Threats and Attacks in the Gaming Industry*, Apress Pocket Guides,
https://doi.org/10.1007/979-8-8688-1492-1_4

Their key differences involve aspects like

- **Nature:** Threats are potential future risks, while attacks are actual events.

- **Focus:** Threats highlight what could go wrong, while attacks demonstrate what has gone wrong or is occurring.

- **Outcome:** Threats may lead to attacks if not mitigated; attacks result in measurable consequences such as data loss, financial damage, or system downtime.

To better understand the differences between threats and attacks:

- A **threat** is like knowing that burglars exist and might target our house.

- An **attack** is when a burglar actually breaks into our house.

Table 4-1 shows the main differences between cybersecurity threats and attacks.

Table 4-1. *Differences between cybersecurity threats and attacks*

Aspect	Cybersecurity threats	Cybersecurity attacks
Definition	A potential danger or risk that could exploit vulnerabilities and cause harm	A deliberate action taken to exploit a vulnerability and cause harm
Nature	Passive—represents a possibility or risk but hasn't necessarily been executed	Active—an actual attempt to compromise security
Examples	Malware, phishing, DDoS risks, zero-day vulnerabilities	Hacking into a system, launching a phishing campaign, executing a DDoS attack
Intent	May or may not have malicious intent (e.g., natural disasters can be threats)	Always intentional, carried out by cybercriminals, hackers, or malicious insiders
Outcome	Could lead to security breaches if not mitigated	Directly causes data breaches, financial loss, or system damage

Understanding these differences is essential for implementing effective cybersecurity strategies. Organizations need to identify and assess threats to prevent attacks, and once an attack occurs, they must have response protocols in place to mitigate damage.

Cybersecurity attacks can impact in many ways on the gaming sector like for instance:

- **Financial Losses:** Attacks can lead to significant financial repercussions due to loss of revenue, repair costs, and potential legal liabilities.

- **User Trust and Loyalty:** Repeated security breaches can erode player trust, reduce player base, and harm the brand's reputation.

- **Regulatory Challenges:** With the rise of regulations regarding data protection, gaming companies face increased scrutiny and potential penalties for failing to safeguard user data.

Let's analyze these cybersecurity threats and attacks in the gaming industry to understand what they are and their impacts and provide a small example.

- **Distributed Denial-of-Service (DDoS) Attacks:**

  What it is:

  Cybercriminals flood gaming servers with excessive traffic, causing disruptions or making the game unplayable.

  Impact:

  - Server downtime and loss of revenue.

  - Frustration among players, leading to declining user engagement.

  Example:

  A major game publisher experiences a DDoS attack during an online tournament, affecting thousands of players.

- **Account Takeover and Credential Stuffing:**

  What it is:

  Hackers use stolen or leaked login credentials to gain unauthorized access to player accounts.

Impact:

- Loss of in-game assets, virtual currency, and personal data.

- Unauthorized purchases or fraudulent transactions.

- Increased risk of identity theft.

Example:

A hacker gains access to thousands of gaming accounts by using leaked passwords from previous data breaches.

- **Cheating and Game Manipulation:**

  What it is:

  Attackers use bots, hacks, and exploits to gain an unfair advantage in competitive gaming.

  Impact:

  - Unbalanced gameplay, causing frustration among legitimate players.

  - Damage to a game's reputation and potential loss of players.

  - Legal action against cheat developers in extreme cases.

  Example:

  Aimbots and wallhacks in first-person shooter games give some players an unfair advantage.

- **Phishing and Social Engineering Attacks:**

What it is:

Cybercriminals impersonate game companies or platforms to trick users into revealing login credentials or personal information.

Impact:

- Loss of accounts, financial information, or sensitive data.

- Potential malware infections through fake downloads.

Example:

Players receive emails claiming they won a free in-game item, leading them to enter their credentials on a fake website.

- **Malware and Ransomware:**

What it is:

Malware is often disguised as game mods, cheats, or pirated copies of games, infecting players' devices.

Impact:

- Data theft and system corruption.

- Ransomware encrypts files, demanding a ransom for decryption.

Example:

A popular game mod contains hidden malware that steals passwords and banking information.

- **Data Breaches and Leaks:**

  What it is:

  Hackers target gaming companies to steal sensitive user data, including names, emails, and payment details.

  Impact:

  - Exposure of millions of user records.

  - Regulatory fines and lawsuits.

  - Loss of customer trust.

  Example:

  A major gaming platform is hacked, exposing user credentials and payment information to the dark web.

- **Supply Chain Attacks:**

  What it is:

  Cybercriminals target third-party developers, tools, or update servers to introduce vulnerabilities in a game.

  Impact:

  - Introduction of backdoors or malware into legitimate software.

  - Potential compromise of game security and player data.

  Example:

  A hacker injects malicious code into a game update, infecting thousands of players' devices.

- **In-Game Fraud and Virtual Item Theft:**

  What it is:

  Fraudsters steal virtual currency, rare items, or scam players into fake trades.

  Impact:

  - Economic imbalance within the game.

  - Financial losses for players and developers.

  Example:

  A scammer tricks a player into trading a rare skin but never delivers the promised in-game currency.

- **Zero-Day Exploits and Game Vulnerabilities:**

  What it is:

  Hackers discover and exploit undisclosed vulnerabilities in game code or infrastructure.

  Impact:

  - Unauthorized access to game servers.

  - Ability to modify game mechanics or steal data.

  Example:

  A vulnerability in a game's authentication system allows attackers to bypass login security.

- **Fake Reviews and Bot Attacks:**

  What it is:

  Attackers manipulate review scores using fake accounts or bots.

Impact:

- Misleading consumers with artificially high or low ratings.

- Unfair competition between game developers.

Example:

A game competitor floods a rival's page with negative bot-generated reviews.

What Is Denial-of-Service (DoS) Attack?

In order to understand in more detail the major cybersecurity attack in the gaming industry, which is the DDoS cybersecurity attack, we must first learn what is the denial-of-service (DoS) attack and how it is different from DDoS.

A **denial-of-service (DoS) attack** is a cyberattack designed to disrupt a website or network by overwhelming it with excessive traffic. Attackers flood the target server with numerous requests, slowing it down or crashing it, preventing access for legitimate users.

A DoS attack aims to make a system, network, or service unavailable by overloading it with fake requests. This prevents real users from accessing resources, leading to slow performance or complete failure.

Here are the most important types of DoS attacks:

1. **Volume-Based Attacks:**

   These attacks flood a network with excessive data, exhausting its bandwidth. Examples:

- **UDP Floods**: Attackers send large volumes of UDP packets to random ports, overwhelming the server.

- **ICMP Floods**: A network is flooded with ICMP packets, disrupting normal operations.

2. **Protocol Attacks:**

These attacks exploit vulnerabilities in network protocols to deplete server resources. Examples:

- **SYN Floods**: Attackers send multiple SYN requests but never complete the handshake, consuming server memory.

- **Ping of Death**: Oversized packets crash the target server.

3. **Application Layer Attacks:**

Target specific applications or services to degrade performance or cause crashes. Examples:

- **HTTP Floods**: Attackers send excessive HTTP requests to exhaust resources.

- **Slowloris**: Keeps connections open by sending incomplete requests, preventing new ones.

4. **Distributed Denial-of-Service (DDoS) Attacks:**

DDoS attacks involve multiple compromised systems (botnets) attacking a single target. Examples:

- **Amplification Attacks**: Small queries generate large responses, overwhelming the victim.

- **Botnet-Based Attacks**: Large networks of infected devices generate attack traffic from multiple locations.

5. **Resource Exhaustion:**

Repeated requests overload a system, causing crashes and making services inaccessible.

6. **Reflective Attacks:**

Attackers manipulate third-party servers to unknowingly send responses to the victim, flooding them with traffic. Examples:

- **DNS Reflection**: Attackers send forged requests to DNS servers, redirecting responses to the victim.

- **NTP Reflection**: Similar attack using Network Time Protocol servers.

What are then the key differences between DoS (denial-of-service) and DDoS (distributed denial-of-service) attacks?

The key difference is measured based on the number of attackers, the scale of the attack, how to detect and mitigate the attacks, and finally the complexity of the attack.

Let's understand them a bit in detail:

1. **Number of Attackers:**

- **DoS Attack:** Initiated by a single system or attacker flooding a target with excessive traffic

- **DDoS Attack:** Uses multiple systems (often a botnet of compromised computers) to attack a target simultaneously, making it harder to stop

2. **Scale and Impact:**

- **DoS:** Smaller in scale, affecting only a single target from a single source

- **DDoS:** Larger and more powerful, with attack traffic coming from multiple locations, making it more difficult to mitigate

3. **Detection and Mitigation:**

- **DoS:** Easier to detect and block since all traffic comes from one source.

- **DDoS:** Harder to prevent because the attack traffic comes from many sources, often using legitimate-looking requests

4. **Attack Complexity:**

- **DoS:** Simpler to execute and usually done using basic scripts or tools

- **DDoS:** More complex, requiring coordination of multiple infected machines (botnets) to execute the attack

So basically, DoS is a one-on-one attack from a single machine, while DDoS is a large-scale attack using multiple devices. Also, DDoS attacks are harder to stop because they originate from multiple sources, making them more disruptive and challenging to block.

Understanding Distributed Denial-of-Service (DDoS) Attack

Let's understand the most typical and critical cybersecurity attack in the gaming industry such as the distributed denial-of-service (DDoS) attack.

A **distributed denial-of-service (DDoS) attack** is a type of cyberattack in which multiple compromised devices (botnets) flood a target system, network, or server with excessive traffic, causing disruptions or making services completely unavailable.

DDoS attacks are a major cybersecurity threat across various industries, including gaming, finance, healthcare, and e-commerce. These attacks can result in server crashes, financial losses, and damage to a company's reputation.

Let's understand now how the DDoS cybersecurity attack works:

1. **Botnet Creation**: Attackers create or rent a botnet, which is a network of compromised computers or devices (bots) that can be controlled remotely. These devices are infected with malware without the owners' knowledge.

2. **Target Selection**: The attacker selects a target, which can be a website, server, or network.

3. **Traffic Overload**: The attacker sends commands to the botnet to flood the target with excessive traffic, overwhelming its resources. This can be done using various methods:

    -   **Volumetric Attacks**: These generate huge amounts of traffic to saturate the bandwidth of the target.

- **Protocol Attacks**: These target weaknesses in the protocols used by the target, like SYN floods that exploit the TCP handshake.

- **Application Layer Attacks**: These focus on specific functions of the web server, such as HTTP requests that require significant processing power to handle.

4. **System Failure**: The target system becomes overloaded, slowing down or crashing completely.

5. **Service Disruption**: Legitimate users cannot access the affected website, game, or online service.

6. **Impact**: As traffic increases, the target server can become slow or unavailable, leading to downtime, loss of revenue, and damage to reputation.

Protection Against Threats and Cybersecurity Attacks in the Gaming Industry

So how can we protect ourselves from the threats and cybersecurity attacks in the gaming industry?

Let's see some examples.

Protection Against DDoS Attacks:

DDoS protection is provided by specific DDoS protection systems which operate continuously, monitoring and mitigating attacks in real time to maintain network security and availability.

These solutions use generally advanced technologies to prevent disruptions:

- **Deep Packet Inspection:** Every incoming data packet is analyzed to distinguish between legitimate traffic and malicious requests, ensuring harmful data is blocked.

- **Network Traffic Monitoring:** By constantly observing traffic patterns, the system establishes a baseline of normal activity, allowing it to quickly detect unusual spikes that may signal a DDoS attack.

- **Adaptive Mitigation Strategies:** When an attack is identified, various countermeasures—such as traffic filtering, rate limiting, and redirecting harmful traffic to scrubbing centers—are deployed to prevent service disruptions while ensuring legitimate users maintain access.

For Game Companies:

- **Deploy DDoS Protection Solutions:** Use services like Cloudflare, AWS Shield, or Akamai to filter malicious traffic.

- **Scalable Infrastructure:** Use cloud-based solutions that can handle sudden spikes in traffic.

- **Traffic Monitoring:** Implement real-time monitoring to detect abnormal activity before it escalates.

For Players:

- Use **VPNs** to hide your real IP address, reducing the risk of direct targeting.

- Play on **official and reputable gaming servers** that have security measures in place.

Preventing Account Takeovers and Credential Stuffing:
For Game Companies:

- **Enforce Multi-factor Authentication (MFA):** Require players to enable MFA for additional security.

- **Implement Strong Password Policies:** Encourage/ require players to use complex passwords.

- **Use CAPTCHA Systems:** Prevent automated bots from attempting mass logins.

For Players:

- Enable **MFA** on gaming accounts.

- Use **unique, strong passwords** for each game or platform.

- Avoid **reusing passwords** across different gaming services.

Stopping Phishing Scams and Social Engineering:
For Game Companies:

- **Educate Users:** Notify players about common phishing scams through official channels.

- **Secure Email and Support Systems:** Use verified email domains to prevent spoofing.

- **Monitor and Remove Fake Websites:** Take legal action against fake game-related phishing sites.

For Players:

- **Avoid Clicking Suspicious Links:** Never enter login credentials on unknown websites.

- **Verify Official Emails:** Only trust emails from official game publishers.

- **Report Phishing Attempts:** If you receive a suspicious email or message, report it to the game developer.

Defending Against Malware and Ransomware:
For Game Companies:

- **Secure Game Files and Updates:** Use encryption and digital signatures to prevent malware injection.

- **Scan and Remove Malicious Mods/Cheats:** Monitor third-party software that interacts with the game.

- **Conduct Regular Security Audits:** Identify and fix security loopholes before they are exploited.

For Players:

- **Download Games Only from Official Sources:** Avoid pirated or unofficial versions.

- **Do Not Install Cheats or Unverified Mods:** Many hacks contain hidden malware.

- **Keep Antivirus Software Up to Date:** Use a reliable security solution to scan for threats.

Preventing Data Breaches and Leaks:
For Game Companies:

- **Encrypt User Data:** Protect sensitive data using strong encryption techniques.

- **Limit Data Collection:** Avoid storing unnecessary personal information.

- **Implement Regular Security Audits:** Assess security vulnerabilities frequently.

- **Use Firewalls and Intrusion Detection Systems:** Monitor network traffic for suspicious activities.

For Players:

- **Limit Personal Data Shared in Games:** Avoid using real names in gaming profiles.

- **Review Privacy Settings:** Adjust in-game privacy settings to restrict data exposure.

- **Be Cautious About Linking Accounts:** Linking gaming accounts (e.g., Steam, PlayStation, Xbox) can increase risk if one is compromised.

Stopping In-Game Fraud and Virtual Item Theft:
For Game Companies:

- **Implement Secure Trade Systems:** Use escrow services for safe item exchanges.

- **Monitor Marketplaces for Fraudulent Transactions:** Detect unusual trading patterns and scam activities.

- **Enforce Strict Anti-fraud Policies:** Ban accounts engaged in fraudulent activities.

For Players:

- **Avoid Third-Party Trading Sites:** Use official in-game marketplaces for transactions.

- **Verify Trades Before Accepting:** Double-check item details before completing transactions.

- **Report Scammers:** If you encounter fraud, report it to the game's support team.

Preventing Cheating and Exploits:

For Game Companies:

- **Use Advanced Anti-cheat Systems:** Implement AI-driven cheat detection tools like Easy Anti-Cheat or BattlEye.

- **Patch Vulnerabilities Regularly:** Release frequent updates to fix game exploits.

- **Enforce Fair Play Policies:** Ban cheaters and take legal action against cheat developers.

For Players:

- **Avoid Using Cheats:** Not only does cheating ruin the game, but it also puts your account at risk.

- **Report Cheaters:** Help maintain fair gameplay by reporting suspicious activities.

- **Play on Secure and Trusted Servers:** Official servers are more secure and actively monitored.

Securing Gaming Supply Chains:

For Game Companies:

- **Vet Third-Party Vendors:** Ensure external partners follow strict security protocols.

- **Secure Update Channels:** Digitally sign game updates to prevent tampering.

- **Monitor Source Code Changes:** Detect any unauthorized modifications to game code.

Cybersecurity Best Practices in the Game Industry

Cybersecurity in the gaming industry is critical due to the sensitive data, intellectual property, and user trust at stake.

Here are some best practices that can help ensure robust security:

1. **Data Protection**:

    - **Encryption**: Use encryption for sensitive data both in transit and at rest to protect against unauthorized access

    - **Data Minimization**: Collect only necessary data to minimize exposure and risk

2. **Secure Development Practices**:

    - **Code Reviews and Audits**: Regularly conduct code reviews and security audits to identify and fix vulnerabilities

    - **Secure Coding Standards**: Follow secure coding guidelines, such as OWASP (Open Web Application Security Project) standards, to prevent common vulnerabilities

3. **Access Management**:

    - **Role-Based Access Control (RBAC)**: Implement RBAC to limit access to sensitive systems and data to only those who need it for their role

    - **Strong Authentication**: Use multi-factor authentication (MFA) for players and employees to enhance security

4. **Network Security**:

- **Firewalls and Intrusion Detection Systems**: Utilize firewalls and intrusion detection systems to monitor and protect network traffic

- **DDoS Protection**: Implement solutions to protect against distributed denial-of-service (DDoS) attacks

5. **Regular Testing and Monitoring**:

- **Penetration Testing**: Conduct regular penetration tests to identify vulnerabilities before they can be exploited

- **Continuous Monitoring**: Use security information and event management (SIEM) systems for real-time monitoring and detection of suspicious activities

6. **User Education and Awareness**:

- **Training**: Provide regular cybersecurity training to employees about social engineering, phishing tactics, and other threats

- **User Best Practices**: Educate players about creating strong passwords and recognizing phishing attempts

7. **Incident Response Plan**:

- **Develop and Test a Response Plan**: Prepare an incident response plan to address potential security breaches quickly and effectively

- **Regular Updates**: Continuously update the plan based on new threats and vulnerabilities

8. **Compliance and Legal Considerations**:

- **Understand Regulations**: Stay informed about relevant regulations, such as GDPR or COPPA, to ensure compliance related to user data and privacy

- **Third-Party Risk Management**: Evaluate and manage the security practices of third-party vendors and partners

Implementing these best practices can help game developers and publishers safeguard their assets and maintain player trust and engagement.

Adopting Secure Software Development Life Cycle (SSDLC) Process

For game developers, it is crucial to make sure the code development is generated following a secure methodology.

One of the most common and used Secure Software Development methodology is named **Secure Software Development Life Cycle (SSDLC)** which is a methodology that integrates security measures and practices into every phase of software development. It ensures that security considerations are addressed early and consistently throughout the entire process, from initial design to deployment and maintenance. This proactive approach helps mitigate security vulnerabilities and ensures that the final product is more resilient to cyber threats.

The Secure Software Development Life Cycle (SSDLC) consists of several phases, each incorporating security practices to ensure the development of secure software.

Here's an overview of the SSDLC process:

1. **Planning and Requirements**

   - Define security requirements based on compliance (e.g., GDPR, ISO 27001, OWASP)

   - Perform risk assessment and threat modeling

   - Establish security policies and guidelines

2. **Design**

   - Threat modeling (identify potential security threats and vulnerabilities)

   - Secure architecture design (use design patterns that enforce security)

   - Select secure technologies and frameworks

3. **Development (Coding)**

   - Follow secure coding practices (e.g., OWASP Secure Coding Guidelines)

   - Use static code analysis tools to detect vulnerabilities

   - Implement input validation, authentication, and encryption mechanisms

4. **Testing**

   - Conduct security testing:

   - Static and dynamic application security testing (SAST & DAST)

- Penetration testing

- Fuzz testing (input randomization to find vulnerabilities)

- Perform code reviews and security audits

5. **Deployment**

- Harden system configurations (secure servers, databases, and APIs)

- Monitor for security threats during deployment

- Use secure deployment practices (e.g., container security, DevSecOps)

6. **Maintenance and Monitoring**

- Continuous security monitoring (SIEM, Intrusion Detection Systems)

- Regular patching and vulnerability management

- Incident response and post-mortem analysis for security breaches

7. **Compliance and Training**

- Ensure ongoing compliance with industry security standards

- Train developers and teams on secure coding and best practices

The gaming industry, particularly the online gaming sector, is a prime target for various cybersecurity threats and attacks. This is due to the massive player base, the value of in-game items and currencies, and the use of online infrastructure for multiplayer experiences.

As we said earlier, the gaming industry faces various cybersecurity threats, including DDoS attacks, phishing scams, data breaches, and in-game fraud. Mitigating these threats requires a combination of security measures, best practices, and awareness initiatives for both players and game developers.

For this reason, the gaming industry must remain vigilant to these threats, as cyberattacks not only affect revenue but can also harm a game's reputation and player trust.

We need to ensure the security of your games and protect both your players and your game's integrity from potential threats. Keep in mind that game security is an ongoing process that requires vigilance and continuous improvement.

Final suggested minimum gaming security steps are as follows:

- Anticipate the **key architecture elements and technologies** in your future game solution to define the needed security measures to adopt

- Define the **security standard and framework** to be adopted in your organization for gaming development

- Make sure you understand the **regulations and legislations** involved in your gaming development solutions

- Follow **cybersecurity best practices** in the gaming development process

- Build Secure Software Development Life Cycle **(SSDLC) process** to be followed

- Scan for vulnerabilities in your game infrastructure by running periodically **penetration testing**

Summary

Cybersecurity threats in the gaming industry can cause major disruptions, financial losses, and damage to reputation. Game developers must implement strong security measures, while players should remain vigilant and follow best practices to protect their accounts and personal data.

In this chapter, we focused on cybersecurity threats and attacks in the gaming industry, especially the DDoS cybersecurity attacks.

We introduced the most common threats and attacks and explained why and how they occur.

We explained in detail the types of cybersecurity attacks in the gaming industry and how to mitigate them and also explained the Secure Software Development Life Cycle (SSDLC) process to develop games in secure ways.

Finally, we highlighted how strengthening security measures, promoting user awareness, and implementing best practices for password management and data protection can help mitigate these threats and attacks.